SHOW-ME WARRIOR

O. K. Armstrong of Missouri

MARTIN CAPAGES JR. PHD

© 2020 Martin Capages Jr.

All rights reserved. No part of this book may be reproduced or utilized in any form or by any means, electronic or mechanical, including photocopying, recording or by any information storage retrieval system without permission in writing from the publisher, except for a reviewer who may quote brief passages in a review to be printed in a newspaper, magazine or electronic publication.

American Freedom Publications LLC

www.americanfreedompublications.com

2638 E. Wildwood Road

Springfield, MO 65804

ISBN 978-1-64764-375-1   Hardback Version

ISBN 978-1-64764-394-2   Paperback Version

ISBN 978-1-64764-411-6   E-book Version

Cover Design Christopher M. Capages

www.capagescreative.com

Manuscript Editor

First Edition- October 2, 2020

Printed in the United States of America

"Peace is not founded upon disarmament; Peace is founded upon liberty and justice." O. K. Armstrong

"Life can be beautiful; It is bountiful, if not always materially, and it is brief. Everyone should try to fix his or her helm on gratitude for life and its blessings, but to do so takes a wakeful watch." Charles Lindbergh Armstrong

DEDICATION

This book is dedicated to the memory of Orland Kay Armstrong, husband, father, freelance journalist, writer, publisher and United States Congressman from the 6th District of Missouri. O. K. Armstrong was a crusader for Justice and warrior for Truth, inspired by his Faith to serve his fellow citizens.

ACKNOWLEDGEMENTS

It has been my distinct honor to develop this biography at the request of the Armstrong Family. It could not have been completed without the direct encouragement and involvement of O. K. Armstrong Jr. ("Kay") and his brothers, Milton and Stanley Armstrong as well as the writings of their youngest brother, the late Dr. Charles Lindbergh Armstrong.

I would also like to acknowledge the encouragement and prayers provided by my wife, Pamela, as well as her recollections of the Armstrong family as fellow members of University Heights Baptist Church in Springfield, Missouri.

TABLE OF CONTENTS

Dedication v
Acknowledgements vi
TABLE OF CONTENTS vii
OTHER WORKS BY THE AUTHOR viii
Foreword ix
Preface xi
Introduction 1
MISSOURI BORN 5
World War One: "The Great War" 9
Post-War Service 15
The move to Florida 20
The Love of His Life 22
Back to Missouri 27
Florida Calls Again 29
The Lindbergh Connection 31
The Lure of the Ozarks 41
Freelance Journalist 43
The Dream House 45
The Great Depression 51
CRUSADER FOR JUSTICE 57
CRUSADER FOR PEACE 63
Louise Armstrong Passing 77
The Changing of the Guard 87
Back to Politics 93
The Korean War 97
The Cold War 125
A Slap at THE SOVIETS 137
Family Complexities 141
Falsely Accused and Vindication 147
EVANGELICAL CRUSADER 151
O.K.'s Post Vietnam War Analysis 159
FINAL COMMENTS 167
ABOUT THE AUTHOR 171
DISCLAIMER 173
BIBLIOGRAPHY AND WORKS CITED 175
NOTABLE BOOKS 176
OTHER REFERENCES 177
INDEX 183

OTHER WORKS BY THE AUTHOR

BOOTS TO BOGIES TO BRONZE: The Authorized World War II Biography of 2LT Jack C. Pyatt

THE MORAL CASE FOR AMERICAN FREEDOM

OZARK COUNTY HEART: Boyhood Memories of a Dora Missouri Farm

A WAKEFUL WATCH: The Authorized Biography of Charles Lindbergh Armstrong

HEARTLAND REBELLION

THE SILENT SECOND: The Biography of Martin Capages- Captain USMC

EPIPHANY: Before Time Zero- Faith of an Engineer

WHY THE GREEN NEW DEAL IS A BAD DEAL FOR AMERICA

FREEDOM OR SOCIALISM? The Millennial Dilemma

STARBOARD TACK: The Free Nation Makes a Course Correction

OF OSTRICHES AND LEMMINGS: The Silliness of Climate Change Hysteria

FOREWORD

By Milton McCool Armstrong, O. K. Armstrong Jr. and William Stanley Armstrong

Our younger brother Charles had many heroes in his background, from our father, Orland Kay (O. K.) Armstrong, our father's famous friend, Charles Lindbergh as well as we three older brothers, Milton, Kay, Stanley and our sister, Louise. Charles was an avid researcher and family historian. He carried on many discussions with our father and documented those in writing. When Charles passed away, we took action to have Charles' biography and his research writings on our family history memorialized by Dr. Martin Capages Jr. and American Freedom Publications LLC. The book entitled *A WAKEFUL WATCH* was the result.

That book reaffirmed our belief that our family was blessed with a father who was a true crusader, a leader with rare courage and clarity of vision, who championed the cause of freedom, democratic government and human rights of peoples near and far.

"The foundation of it all was a mission that he was destined to have some important role in bettering the country. Bettering its people, the world, too. But he didn't see his mission as being an evangelist; it wasn't that. It was more like evangelism of democracy, freedom and liberty." *Milton McCool Armstrong.*

"It was amazing to watch Dad speak to an audience. He would have the audience fall in love with him and his words and be swayed by them." *O. K. Armstrong Jr.*

"Our dad hated war and always opposed what he deemed to be a senseless intervention into a foreign war. But when he came to the

Vietnam Conflict, his opinion was, 'if the United States had to fight a war, then let's win it.' Dad told a reporter in 1966, 'Every possible military means should be taken to win the war in Vietnam as soon as possible.' One of the most important and useful lessons I learned from my father was that he was comfortable around anybody, rich, poor, religious, non-religious, Democrat, Republican, and I adopted it in my life." *William Stanley Armstrong.*

A close friend to the Armstrong family for almost 50 years, Dr. Durward G. Hall (also a U. S. Congressman from Missouri) would say:

"O. K. Armstrong was a flamboyant person who was likely to draw lightning and fire. He was a great man who contributed to his community and served well the people he represented. He paid all possible rent for the space he occupied on Earth."

PREFACE

Orland Kay Armstrong was a man of great character and discipline. A native of Missouri, his lifetime encompassed many events and he accomplished much. However, as with most reluctant heroes, his story has been essentially untold. When I was asked to develop the biography of O. K. Armstrong's youngest son, Charles Lindberg Armstrong, I was initially overwhelmed by the sheer mental capacity of this younger son of the U. S. Congressman from Missouri. Over the course of the research and writing of the son's story, I became intrigued by the underlying story of Charles's father. Charles writings were the starting point for telling the real and complex story of the Show-Me State's heroic, but often crusading warrior, the Honorable Orland Kay Armstrong.

From the original material reviewed, to include handwritten editorial comments made by his brother, Kay, on Charles' typewritten text, this family was extraordinary in their love for one another. However, I would be remiss if I did not mention the Scottish heritage of this family as related to me by Kay Armstrong. The Armstrong Clan were the defenders of the Scottish Borders. They were an exceedingly rough bunch with a reputation for greatness in battle that was tarnished by a tendency toward brutality and criminality. The motto of the Armstrong Clan is, "I remained unvanquished," and their coat of arms is presented in a fitting manner on the cover of this book.

Charles Armstrong had a wonderful way with words and phrases. One that I became particularly fond of relates well to this noble American family. *"Life can be beautiful; It is bountiful, if not always materially, and it is brief. Everyone should try to fix his or her helm on gratitude for life and its blessings, but to do so takes a wakeful watch."*

Orland Kay Armstrong was referred to as "O. K.," by his friends. According to his younger son Charles, his father "exemplified that the fundamental personality is delivered with the baby and that individuals are alloys of genetic ore fused and tempered in the crucible of experience. For him, leadership was an inborn and life-defining trait, evident to all during his first decade of life, and a positive pole to the negative one of my grandfather 'Calvin's personal weaknesses. My father's relatives, friends, colleagues, acquaintances, associates and enemies were unanimous: They had never known a more natural leader. As one of them put it, 'O. K. led, and if somebody didn't like it, he led anyway.'" Charles would relate that his father was "a crusader who never had much to do with doubt, but who more than once failed to seize the moment."

The contribution of O. K. Armstrong has gone unrecognized even in the state of his birth, Missouri. Here you have a man who fought for the recognition of African-Americans as equal citizens before there was a Civil Rights movement. He brought to the forefront the plight of Native Americans and proposed corrective actions. He went out of his way to treat all races and creeds evenly and to correct injustice. He stood up to the Soviet Union and was swatted down by the mainstream press and his own political party. He has been essentially overlooked as an American hero. Consider the School of Journalism at the University of Missouri in Columbia. This journalism school is one of the oldest formal journalism schools in the world. Today, the School provides academic education and practical training in all areas of journalism and strategic communication for undergraduate and graduate students across several media including television and radio broadcasting, newspapers, magazines, photography, and new media. The school also supports a robust advertising and public relations curriculum. I am proud to say that both my sister Cheryl and my granddaughter Jordan are graduates of the University of Missouri School of Journalism.

The school opened on September 14, 1908. Its founding was urged by Joseph Pulitzer, following lobbying by Walter Williams, the editor of the Columbia (Missouri) Herald and a university curator. Williams became the official founder of the University of Missouri School of Journalism and would go on to become the President of the University.

In 1981, the school was ranked the top journalism school in the country. It is an outstanding school that touts some notable alumni. While the list includes a former U.S. Representative from Texas's 24th district and two movie stars (including Academy Award winner Brad Pitt), it does not include the Congressman from Missouri's 6th District, a graduate from Mizzou's School of Journalism whose mentor was Walter Williams, a man selected by Williams to found the University of Florida's School of Journalism, and a man who would become the Reader's Digest most prolific journalist and investigative reporter in history. To date, The University of Missouri School of Journalism does not show O. K. Armstrong as a notable alumnus. This book is intended to set the record straight.

Much of the material in this chronical of O. K. Armstrong was previously published in the biography of Charles Lindbergh Armstrong entitled A WAKEFUL WATCH that was published in 2018. Following that publication, more information on Orland Kay Armstrong has become available from the Armstrong family and from the Repository of The State Historical Society of Missouri. Some of that additional material has been included in SHOW-ME WARRIOR.

Martin Capages Jr. PhD
Author of A WAKEFUL WATCH

CHAPTER 1
INTRODUCTION

One key to the Armstrong story is the relationship of O. K. Armstrong, to the famous Lone Eagle, Charles Augustus Lindbergh (or Lucky Lindy). This will be discussed in later paragraphs and Chapters 9 and 15 of this book. The son of a southern Missouri minister, Orland Kay Armstrong graduated *summa cum laude* from Drury College in Springfield, Missouri. He was also a flyer and had served as a pilot during World War One. After the war, he earned his law degree at Cumberland University in Tennessee, and went on to earn a master's degree in journalism from the University of Missouri, studying under Walter Williams, the Dean of the University of Missouri School of Journalism. He then moved to Florida.

Orland Kay Armstrong 1961

CHAPTER 1   INTRODUCTION

In Florida, O. K. Armstrong continued his string of successes. In fact, Walter Williams came to the University of Florida to install Armstrong as the first head of the University's Department of Journalism. The 1928 University yearbook, the Seminole, reported: "The College of Commerce and Journalism was established as the School of Business and Journalism in 1925. For the first year it operated under the College of Arts and Sciences with the Dean of the College in charge. Beginning with the first semester of 1926 a special director was appointed, and the School began to operate as a unit separate from the College of Arts and Sciences. In the Spring of 1927, the Board of Control created the College of Commerce and Journalism out of this unit with a dean and faculty of its own and made it co-equal in every respect with the other colleges of the University.

O. K. Armstrong had also worked as a freelance journalist for several newspapers and national magazines in the mid-1920s. Returning to Missouri in 1929, O. K. first entered politics the next year in an unsuccessful run for a seat in the state senate. Armstrong tried again in 1932 and, in a year dominated by Democratic landslides from the White House to the state house, he became one of only ten Republicans elected to the Missouri House of Representatives. He would serve in the House until 1936 and then again from 1942 to 1944. Armstrong would continue his journalism career even while in the state legislature, some of his reporting would have national ramifications. One article, which gained him notoriety, was a rare 1927 interview with Charles Lindbergh for Boys' Life magazine. After that interview, the two aviators, both with Missouri ties, became close friends. They would work together as patriots with a vision to keep the United States out of another world war. In this endeavor they would be unsuccessful, but not due to their own actions.

It would be History that would have the final say. The Japanese attack on Pearl Harbor on December 7, 1941 would change both Lindbergh's and Armstrong's position on the matter.

O. K. Armstrong was elected to serve one term in the U.S. House of Representatives for Missouri from January 1951 to January 1953. He also received many other honorary degrees before he passed away on April 15, 1987, in Springfield, Missouri.

"Until his health waned in his 90s, O. K. Armstrong would lead all sizes of crusades, with themes such as integrity vs. governmental corruption; peace-the health of nations and international relations, which he believed to be founded on liberty and justice; and moral strength--to him the rule of the road toward fulfillment in life." (Charles L. Armstrong)

CHAPTER 2

MISSOURI BORN

Orland Kay "O. K." Armstrong was born on October 2, 1893 in Willow Springs, Missouri, the third of nine children. His father, Reverend William Calvin Armstrong, was a schoolteacher and minister. Calvin was born June 19, 1861 in the town of Lexington in Lafayette County, Missouri. He passed away on February 10, 1947 in Springfield, Greene County Missouri. O. K.'s mother, Calvin's wife, was Ternitia Agnes Brockus Armstrong. She was born on November 1, 1866 in Polk County, Missouri. Agnes passed away on October 16, 1951, also in Springfield, Missouri. O. K. Armstrong's roots were therefore firmly planted in the Show-Me State.

The family moved frequently around southern Missouri as the Reverend Calvin Armstrong changed teaching jobs or founded new churches. Finally, in 1907 the family settled in Carterville, Missouri and it was from Carterville High School that the young Orland graduated as valedictorian in 1912.

The family then decided on Springfield as home because, as southern Missouri's largest town, its schools were theoretically better than the more rural ones. Calvin, would board the Saturday train to church, taking advantage of the clergy-discount, and return on Sunday evening. During the school year 1911-1912, a Professor McMurtry was sent by the administration of Drury College in Springfield to scout for good students. On the list proposed by the faculty at Carterville High were O. K. and his sister Delta. Delta should have entered college in 1909 but was obliged to sit out those years at home, holding books to her nose, until the family could save enough to buy spectacles. As Valedictorian of the Carterville High School Class of 1912, O. K. was awarded a tuition scholarship from Drury College of Springfield. The Assemblies of God gave him still another scholarship as the child of a minister [of any denomination]. These two grants covered O. K.'s tuition and some living expenses his first year, a favorable development since the cost of small private schools was out of range for his family: Most of Calvin and Agnes Armstrong's children became missionaries, either officially (to Brazil), or by way of institutional leadership, as, for example, in the Women's Christian Temperance Union, charities, church, and politics from local to national level. But all of them knew that O. K. was the real leader.

O. K. graduated summa cum laude from Drury in 1916. His sister, Delta had graduated summa cum laude from Drury the previous year. Southwest Baptist College in Bolivar, Missouri immediately offered him a position teaching history. Having not yet heard a clear professional call, he accepted. At the sound of the opening bell in September, the college administration reasoned that O. K.'s baccalaureate degree in psychology warranted his teaching that subject as well. O. K. agreed with enthusiasm. But there was more to that first assignment than meets the eye. There were family connections. Southwest Baptist was a natural fit for the young graduate Armstrong for it was his maternal grandfather, Reverend Daniel Preston, who was one of the college founders.

Soon thereafter, Dean Pike observed to O. K. in an aside that "someone was needed to teach the dozen or fifteen novice preachers in whatever else you want them to learn." O. K.'s response to this rather direct hint was the 1916 equivalent of "Oh sure, no problem." Part of "whatever else you want them to learn" was a survey of European-

American history emphasizing the evolution of democratic government, with special emphasis on the U.S. founding. O. K., capable as he was, was not an expert in all those subjects at age twenty-two. But their less-than- fastidious observance of official credentialing (If you can teach something, then go right ahead) and their consequent acceptance of O. K. as an instructor in several fields speaks for the era's relative casualness of academic structure, at least in small college America. "Oh, and by the way, O. K., would you mind taking charge as dean of the dormitory and the forty-five students housed there? We can't finance it, but you just apportion out your costs to the boys residing and boarding there and charge them as much."

"Yes, I believe I can manage that readily."

And again, Dean Pike just a few days later, "Incidentally, O. K., we want to continue some athletics here at Southwest. Have you had any basketball experience?" "Oh, by all means," said O. K., "my brother and I were stars of the second string in high school, and I would be delighted." O. K. recruited six men, giving him always one reserve. They won some games that year against distant powerhouses, such as Buffalo (the one in Missouri), Drury College and Springfield's Normal College (later known as Southwest Missouri State Teachers' College, then Southwest Missouri State University and now, Missouri State University).

Two months into the semester, Dean Pike said, "Now, O. K., we have run out of money. We can't pay you, but can you stay anyhow?" O. K. appealed to his family in Springfield for survival-sufficient funds and stayed the year. He and the boys at the dorm ordered much of their staple foods from Sears and Roebuck, whose prices beat the local suppliers, wholesale or retail.

CHAPTER 3

WORLD WAR ONE: "THE GREAT WAR"

On April 6, 1917, war was declared. The Armstrong boys' grandfather, veteran of two wars, had told them, "If war is declared by the United States, don't wait to be drafted. A conscript will be looked upon as a convict." O. K.'s younger brother Angus signed up on April 9, 1917 and was on the train to Jefferson Barracks in St. Louis that night. Four thousand young men had already gathered. The response had been too great to process. These men were inducted and sent back home to wait to be summoned for training. Meanwhile, Angus volunteered for civilian work as an electrician at the Ship Yard in Philadelphia. There the Navy was converting interned German passenger ships (ships in our waters when war was declared). Angus was assigned to a ship named the U.S.S. von Steuben in honor of the German General whose help was crucial to America's Revolutionary War victory. In August, Angus was ordered to basic infantry training at Camp Clark in Missouri. "We put those new khaki uniforms on and strutted around there like we were some-body. And when we were given our Springfield rifles, we thought we were ready to whip the Kaiser right now. We rode the troop train to Camp Sill Oklahoma, a two-day trip because of stops at every town to pick up more men and more cars."

Angus Armstrong

CHAPTER 3   WORLD WAR ONE

Upon completion of training in the spring of 1918, the men were notified that they would be the unit assigned a new weapon, the machine gun. This was an upsetting development. They knew nothing about the weapon, but this was an infantry unit, and they assumed this turn of events was equivalent to a demotion. How surprised they were to learn the contrary, that they had impressed some visiting brass enough to be awarded this prestigious duty and were no longer "regular infantry."

In May 1918, the well-trained men of Camp Sill started the six-day train trip to New York, and on to Camp Mills for fitting out with new equipment. Then a ferry to New York, where Angus and his 35th Division buddies boarded the steamship Carpathia, which in 1912 had picked up the survivors of the Titanic.

Their convoy of twelve troop ships crossed the Atlantic with anti-sub destroyer escorts patrolling a 180-degree arc before the transports. The sub threat was serious enough that the convoy detoured north of Ireland and came down the channel to Liverpool. "The English lassies welcomed us with open arms, but it was a hug and a goodbye." From Liverpool, they took trains to Southampton, where they boarded ships for Le Havre.

There to greet the disembarking men was a Scottish bagpipe and drum corps. It was the opinion of the high command that the best thing to instill the fighting spirit was the skirl of the Scottish pipes, the martial sound of the drums and the flourish of the kilted marchers. On the sides of the boxcars of the French trains was painted *Quarante Hommes ou Huit Chevaux* (Forty Men *or* Eight Horses). To quote Angus: "We travelled with eight horses *and* forty men. We didn't care. By then we were inured to military orders. If they said give, we gave." In the next war, American troops would travel in those same boxcars. (Capages Jr., 2018)

On the way to Mulhouse the Americans were billeted in villages and farms close to the front, such as St. Mihiel and Thann in Alsace-Lorraine, mostly sharing barns with livestock. Angus and his buddies first came under fire at Thann, a few miles northwest of Mulhouse. They tried to shoot down the German planes that flew over dropping bombs but got no hits. General Black Jack Pershing's plan was to push back the Germans' St. Mihiel salient (50 kilometers northwest of Nancy), part of their thrust to take Paris. And that's what these men did with about two days of intense fire. They then expected some rest time, but it wasn't to be. Next was the annihilation of the Hindenburg Line. General Pershing assigned this task to the 35th Division on Sept. 25, 1918. Angus and his buddies trudged up Hill 285 and set up their machine guns as close side by side as possible in order to lay down a barrage (Angus's word). A naval Lt. Commander approached and told them he had a Navy 16" gun mounted on a flat car, and the signal for the artillery and machine-gun cover for the 'jump off' would be the firing of that gun. Angus: "We woke up with a start as the boom shook the ground at 0500 on Sept. 26. We made a dash for our machine guns and laid down our barrage for the infantry while they jumped off over their trenches and rolled on ahead. Later, our rifle-infantry comrades told us, 'With your machine gun barrage backing us up, we thought our brigade could thrash the whole German army.' Our push against that salient was a turning point in closing the war and forcing the armistice. By October 4, we had pushed their line back by perhaps 20 kilometers; we knew victory was at hand." Angus would suffer during a German gas attack and be sent home. But he was from tough stock, the Armstrong clan, and would live to age 97.

CHAPTER 3   WORLD WAR ONE

Meanwhile back home at the close of the 1916-1917 school year, Dean Pike asked O. K. if he could stay another year, to which O. K. said, "No, I'd rather enlist than be drafted." In an act of wartime patriotism, the YMCA was offering its summer camps to the Army for training purposes. Before O. K. could report to an enlistment station, the Army asked if he would like to be the civilian director of the Keystone National Guard Division, the 28th, consisting of Pennsylvania boys and officers, stationed at the YMCA camp in Augusta, Georgia. The camp was divided into "huts", one for each regiment of men. The 109th and 110th Regiments made up a brigade, the 111th and 112th a second brigade, with a Brigadier for each of those and a Major General over the Division. At these Army training camps and posts most of these young men heard their first Gramophone records, with such hits as "If I Were Huckleberry Finn" and "Let Me Call You Sweetheart" played on a Victor Talking Machine.

O. K. became restless at the National Guard camp. Being civilian and free to do so, he enlisted in the U.S. Army Signal Corps, Aviation unit. While in college, O. K. had learned drill as part of the athletic program. Within a day of reporting as an enlistee to his squadron in Memphis, the Sergeant Major chanted, "If any of you men has ever had military drill, step three paces forward." O. K. alone stepped forward and was promoted to sergeant a few hours later. O. K. began teaching drill the next day and continued to do so for some months. He was transferred to the University of Illinois for special training in administrative skills needed to organize the new branch of the army, the Aviation Detachment. He then returned to his squadron, which had moved from Memphis to Alabama's Taylor Field, now Maxwell Air Force Base but then just a converted cotton patch.

What a change of atmosphere from Champaign-Urbana, where the men went out at night to see the aurora borealis. Now it was semi-tropics balmy. Using shovels, hand scrapers and ox teams hitched to wagons, Negroes leveled the cotton rows into runways for biplanes. Generations later, O. K.'s ear harkened to the singing of these laborers as one of the more pleasant and indelible memories of the Great War era.

Within days of returning from Illinois, O. K. was promoted to sergeant major. He was also assigned to edit *The Propeller*, the newspaper of army aviation. He then took required tests for promotion, passed them, and was commissioned a 2nd Lieutenant.

The Army had a need, a way of finding someone who could fill it, and an award of commensurate rank. Things were a little simpler in those days. The commanding officer at Taylor Field had further reason not to be fussy about army protocol. He was busy inventing a silk cloth and rope device that flyers could strap to their backs to catch the wind after jumping from an airplane, crippled or burning after taking a hit. It was something of an irony for the General that he witnessed, a few days before the armistice, the descent by parachute of the only World War I pilot on either side who could thank the new device for his life--a German, who lost a dogfight to an American but won the

Second Lieutenant O. K. Armstrong

CHAPTER 3   WORLD WAR ONE

privilege of describing this distinction. The General captured the pilot, perhaps a small consolation. Meanwhile, the British command refused to let their men use parachutes on the theory that the new contraptions would sap the flyers' fighting spirit.

With the assignment of rank, O. K. received a new order: report to Chanute Field, Illinois, whither O. K. headed by train. There, late October 1918, the Colonel interrupted O. K.'s preparations for flight training.

The command staff needed an assistant adjutant, someone who was good with a pen. As assistant adjutant, O. K. had access to all orders coming through the field headquarters. One order read, "Find forty-two junior officers to proceed to Kelly Field, Texas, to train the recruits in the aviation section." This meant a nation-wide canvas.

The job was done "mostly by telegraph, perhaps some by mail. Any by telephone would have required a relay of at least four connecting 'central' operators for each call." O. K. and his senior officers mustered, by the first week in November, the quota of junior officers. Inductees from all over the country were set to take the train to Kelly Field for flight training. On the morning of Nov. 11, 1918, a telegram arrived from Washington: "The war is over. Dismiss your recruits".

CHAPTER 4

POST-WAR SERVICE

O. K. was discharged at Taylor Field in February 1919, but, perhaps in gratitude for his promotions, he kept the army informed of his whereabouts in case he was needed. Within a few weeks he received a wire inviting him to don his uniform and direct the Army's YMCA training camp in Springfield, Illinois. There was no more Great War, but there was still a modem army to maintain. As soon as he said "Yes", the army came back with another proposal, or more likely, directive. Go to France and oversee the Russian soldiers liberated from German prison camps and now under the custody of French officers who crave only the ease of nominal command and want someone to take de facto charge of these men. The Russians were freely encamped at Raon l'Etape, 75 kilometers southeast of Nancy. Most of them had been confined to German prison farms where they worked raising food for the German army. As soon as the armistice was signed, the Germans dumped them over into France. Having heard about Bolshevism, France's leader Monsieur Clemenceau inferred that keeping the Russian soldiers in France would be the only humane choice if the alternative was to turn them over to the Bolsheviks for likely execution. The Russians stayed gladly.

While passing through to coordinate plans and orders, the ranking officer said, "Lt. Armstrong, you'll need to linger in Paris a couple of weeks. While you're here, take charge of this boxing tournament we're having for the entertainment of the men still tidying things up before going home." A few days later O. K. presented a token trophy to the

CHAPTER 4   POST-WAR SERVICE

winner of the tournament, a marine named Gene Tunney. Then on to Raon l'Etape, where three thousand Russian soldiers stayed under the coordinated auspices of the U.S. Army and the YMCA. The Army lent O. K. a camionette, a stretch Model T Ford, that had been used as an ambulance during the war. Painted on the side of this little lorry was "American Field Service, Columbia University Class of 1886," the alumni who had raised the money to provide it.

The Russians, "most of them big, burly fellows," were assigned to eight different camps. O. K.'s job was to tour these camps daily in his ambulance to make sure the men were properly fed, kept busy, entertained, and lodged as comfortably as possible given these conditions. The Army Corps of Engineers of World War I had not been called on to do projects of World War II or Vietnam scope, such as building comfortable casernes or barracks. One group of Russians, St. Petersburg cathedral singers quartered together in order to practice their art, was billeted in a barn, not a good likeness to their accustomed prewar lodging. In O. K.'s words, "Oh, what they could do with chords. And what magnificent dancers they were." They played balalaikas (a triangular Russian stringed instrument with a neck like a guitar) they had made from pine boards. To simulate more properly Russian dance by couples, two men of average size volunteered to dance the women's part with husky partners. Now they needed costumes "pour les Dames." Meanwhile, they called upon O. K. to round up more instruments. He filled both orders through Army-YMCA headquarters in Paris. The YMCA, despite the "M" and its military mission, provided some YWCA services and had women's costumes. Through proper channels, of course, O. K. liberated clarinets, flutes, a trumpet, a tambourine, a cello, two fiddles, and pretty frocks for the crossdressers. Nobody could have been more appreciative than those Russian music and dance men in an alien land.

The army sent to O. K. "flickers" (silent movies from Santa Barbara and Hollywood) with French subtitles. The Russian officers were all educated, which to a Russian meant familiarity with French. The movies were a delightful novelty for all and certainly for the Russians. Having been prisoners of the German army for an average of nearly three years, they also knew substantial German. But the Russian officers were still loyal to the Czar and, therefore, refused to speak German. The enlisted men were indifferent or hostile to the Czar and enjoyed practicing the German they had learned in confinement, a happy state for all since O. K. wanted to learn German. O. K. ate alternatively with the Russian officers and enlisted men, and so he had daily classes in French and German.

O. K. Armstrong (center) in France following the end of WWI

CHAPTER 4   POST-WAR SERVICE

After returning from France in 1920 Armstrong chose to further his education at Cumberland University, earning his second bachelor's degree and a law degree in 1922. Armstrong took and passed the Missouri Bar exam but chose not to enter into a law practice. He instead enrolled in the University of Missouri, where he earned both a bachelor's and master's degree in Journalism in 1925.

CHAPTER 5

THE MOVE TO FLORIDA

Even before O. K. and Angus entered the army, their father had looked forward to alleviating his annual Missouri-winter "grippe" by moving south. This hope made him even more than customarily prey to the charms of an oily charlatan. A traveling land-shark named Alyea, peddling his worthless contracts mostly to preachers throughout northern Dixie and the mid-west, moved in on his prey. The Rev. Mr. Armstrong, as pointed out, never suspected anyone would tell him an untruth and was ripe for picking. The smooth-talking con-man depicted for Calvin the charms of some imaginary land on Crystal River at Homosassa on Florida's west coast. Mr. Alyea further "let Calvin in" ("Now Rev. Armstrong, bein' as it's you, tell ya what I'm gonna do ....) on a business deal promoted as if it would allow him, upon his arrival in Florida and with minimal effort, enough monthly income to semi-retire. On this, at least, Alyea had signed promissory notes.

And on that package Calvin blew their meager savings, including some of Agnes's portion of a modest inheritance that had been distributed to each child of Daniel Brockhaus. Included in the deal was the transference to Mr. Alyea of Calvin's Missouri property, which Alyea resold within days.

O. K., just back from France in January 1920, took the Southern Railroad from New York to Florida. He expected to find the family perfectly content in America's semi-tropical Eden. There was much about Florida in those days that was indeed close to paradise. In Crystal's words, "It was as primitive as when the Spanish found it. The rivers were brim with fish --they were jumping out at us. There were no roads. Unless towns were important enough to be connected by railroad, you couldn't get from one to the next without an ox." But O. K. found the family far from content:

"When I arrived down there I said, 'Now Papa, what about your business arrangement? Are they paying you?'

'Well, no; Mr. Alyea says they'll get around to it when the chits come in.' My heart sank. I didn't want to scold my father, but I knew he had been taken."

O. K. tracked down the "skunk" who had pulled this enormity on his father.

O. K.: "This Mr. Alyea was smooth and knew how to worm around. You see, these land sharks would go to the court house and find out what properties' taxes hadn't been paid. I mean, who would want Florida land anyhow? The state capital was up north in Tallahassee because no sane man would ever want to go farther south, where there was nothing but swamps, 'gators and mosquitos. So, they would let the land just lie there. But I was a little wet behind the ears. If I had known then what I know now, I would have taken the buzzard to court."

Ignorant of legal options, O. K. had to settle for telling the serpentine Alyea what he thought of him. For Papa Armstrong a pastorate at nearby-Lake Butler was offered and accepted. And in time this dark interval yielded to a brighter outlook for Calvin's children, who, with one exception, met their betrothed in their new home, the South.

CHAPTER 6
THE LOVE OF HIS LIFE

O. K. had elected to attend law school, but for the sake of filling in the time until the beginning of the next academic year, accepted an offer to become the first director of the Baptist Young People's Union headquartered in Jacksonville, Florida. This job meant travel throughout the southeast. O.K.'s memory was clear sixty-one years later in an interview with his son, Charles:

"On the second Sunday of August (1920), I had returned from business in Birmingham and was free to attend the First Baptist Church of Jacksonville, my headquarters town. During the service, I noticed a beautiful young woman, brunette, with bluish-gray eyes. I was too shy to approach her directly. At the close of the service, I left by the front door and was saying goodbye to an acquaintance on the lower step when suddenly she appeared. To my surprise and delight, she stepped up, extended her hand, and said: 'I know who you are; You're O. K. Armstrong, and if nobody's going to introduce us, I will. I'm Louise McCool.' I was elated. After several minutes of pleasant exchange, I said: 'I must meet you again.' She thought a moment and said, 'I have a little time tomorrow morning'. She set it for 10 am. Believe me, that was one engagement I was anxious to keep.

When we met the next morning, all I could do was just wonder 'How could anybody be as beautiful as this girl is?' I had business about ten blocks away, so I said: 'If you can take the time, I'd like you to walk with me to a publisher's office downtown (Jacksonville) where I must turn in some copy.' She said she'd be delighted, so we strolled together into town. After a dinner and a lunch or two with her that week, we both had out of town obligations to meet. We agreed to meet at the train station in Blackshear on Friday, a few days before she would finish visiting her family in Blackshear and leave for school in Louisville. Louise introduced me to her family, all of whom were there except her older brother, who had married soon after returning from the war in Europe. That evening Louise and I took the train the thirty-five miles to Jessup, where we would take the trolley for Jacksonville. She suggested we walk around Jessup for a while.

Louise McCool in 1920

CHAPTER 6 THE LOVE OF HIS LIFE

While we were walking along in the dusk, some young men walked by and greeted Louise as a longtime friend. We had some friendly back-and-forth, and then one of them said, 'Look, Louise, is this the man you're going to marry?' She said 'Yes, if he'll have me.' Although I didn't say so at the moment, I was smitten. I knew she was the girl for me.

During that school term, we corresponded every few days. In May 1921, we met at a student convention in Chattanooga. Meanwhile, I had heard by way of my sister Crystal, who roomed down the hall from Louise in the dorm at Louisville, that Louise had received more proposals than she could count from the student ministers at the seminary. We took the trolley car that ran from town to the summit of Seminary Ridge. The Civil War history of Seminary Ridge was not my interest of the moment; my mind was on this beautiful girl. There we sat on a big rock as the lights came out on the city below us. There I proposed, and she said: 'I've been waiting for that.'

Soon after that I resigned from my job in Jacksonville to enter the Cumberland University School of Law while Louise completed her studies at Louisville. Louise always thought of that as 'Our lost year.' On May 21, 1922, we were married at the church where we had met. The emeritus pastor who had baptized Louise and her father the Rev. A. M. McCool co-presided. We were happy for 26 years until she was taken from me and from us." O. K. and Louise were a good team.

According to Charles, "I felt secure getting introduced to life in the atmosphere of their mutual regard and affection. I was always pleased that others' accounts of their marriage reaffirmed my entirely positive memories. I idealized their sweethearts' bond, though as an adult I became able to acknowledge my aunt Lois's earthbound observation, "Even your mother and O. K. had to work at it."

O. K. and Louise Armstrong in front of Drury University Chapel, Springfield, Missouri

Louise and O. K. Armstrong in 1947

CHAPTER 7
BACK TO MISSOURI

After O. K.'s graduation the couple settled in Springfield, Missouri, where he passed the bar exam and opened a private practice. As the months wore on it became clear to O. K. that he was uncomfortable in the legal profession, or perhaps uncomfortable with how it was practiced in the real world. By late 1922, he knew that practicing law was not for him. "I was so unhappy and dissatisfied. Soon Louise said, 'Then let's do something else.'" But countering this restless drag were two forward thrusts: journalism and public service.

First and foremost, among the legitimate schools of journalism was the University of Missouri at Columbia, which O. K. entered the semester starting January 1923. Walter Williams, dean and father of modern journalism education in America, had never graduated from any college.

Later, the self-taught dean's career would be crowned as the President of the University of Missouri at Columbia. Academic protocol in those days was undoubtedly much like that of the military; a) Find the most capable person for the position; b) and then assign proportionate credentials.

In 1924, O. K. and his fellow students took a five-week field trip to Nebraska and the Dakotas to gain experience in investigative journalism. One story they compiled during the trip was about plan of the U. S. Postal Service to experiment with hiring aviators to transport the mail. The first air routes would be St. Louis to Chicago and St. Louis to Omaha and a few points farther west. The St. Louis-Chicago route would be

CHAPTER 7   BACK TO MISSOURI

assigned to a young pilot named Charles Lindbergh. Just outside Omaha at a field flat enough to serve as a landing site, the students witnessed and reported the nation's first touchdown of U. S. air mail.

O. K. graduated July 22, 1925, the day after the birth of their first child, Milton. After the conferring of diplomas, Dean Williams quipped, "O. K., this week both you and your wife have earned master's degrees," and then pointed out, "You are now prepared to teach journalism. There are two universities that want you to start a school: Washington and Lee, in Virginia, and the University of Florida." O. K. chose Florida.

During an address to the Florida Press Association convening in Gainesville in early 1925, Dean Williams emphasized journalism as an essential discipline for any school having serious pretensions of being a modern university. The publicizing of this speech bolstered the hopes of the University of Florida's president, A.A. Murphree, who wanted to institute a school of journalism separate from the College of Arts and Sciences. The University's Board of Control approved. Now President Murphree needed a dean for the new college. A tuition fee of ten dollars financed the hiring of Professor (of Economics) Walter Matherly from the University of North Carolina as dean of the College of Business Administration and Journalism. Dean Williams told President Murphree he had just the man in O. K. Armstrong as founding director of journalism education at the new school.

CHAPTER 8

FLORIDA CALLS AGAIN

In July 1925, O. K., Louise and their infant Milton made the two-week trip in their Model T to Gainesville, where O. K. and Professor Matherly founded the School of Journalism at the University of Florida. At the 50th anniversary reunion ceremonies [in 1975], O. K. reminded the guests that in 1925 there were fewer than 2,000 students total at the University of Florida, fewer than the number of faculty in 1975. In 1925, the university comprised fifteen buildings. Students paid a twenty-six-dollar student activity fee, six-dollar infirmary fee, eight-dollar registration fee (tuition), and, for seniors, a five-dollar diploma fee.

O. K. taught eight courses: History and Principles of Journalism; Editorials; Law of the Press; Feature Writing; Newspaper Production; News: Principles of Reporting; News: Practice in Reporting; and Agricultural Journalism. In 1926 O. K. was promoted to Associate professor. With the new title came new obligations (in addition to the usual courses). He would now teach the Writing of Special Articles; The Writing of Feature Articles; Newspaper Management; Industrial and Trade Journalism; Mechanics of Publishing; and a graduate course, Research in Journalism. Among his students was Fuller Warren, future governor of Florida. Even at this time, Warren let everyone know that he intended to be the Governor of Florida someday. O. K. was also Fuller Warren's teacher at another place in Gainesville, his Sunday School class.

CHAPTER 8   FLORIDA CALLS AGAIN

In 1924 the Florida legislature opened the university to women, provided they were at least twenty-one years of age, juniors, and taking courses not offered at any other Florida institution. In 1927 several women enrolled in the school, now called the College of Commerce and Journalism.

CHAPTER 9
THE LINDBERGH CONNECTION

In early June 1927, O. K. set an example for his students. He went to Washington to cover Charles Lindbergh's return from his famous flight. He described the occasion this way:

"President Calvin Coolidge sent the Navy destroyer Memphis to bring the young flyer, at that time the most popular hero of the world, and his plane back home. In New York there was the biggest ticker-tape parade ever held, before or since, down the streets of New York. Then Lindbergh was whisked to Washington to be the guest of President and Mrs. Coolidge at the temporary White House, known as the "McLean House," on DuPont Circle. (The White House was undergoing repairs at the time.) "I was teaching journalism at the University of Florida It was vacation time, so I took a train to Washington to see the big show. On the evening of June 9, I mingled with the huge crowd in a park south of the White House. We watched the Postmaster General, surrounded by all the cabinet, mount a wooden platform and present a special medal to the tall, handsome young hero in honor of his contribution to the new national service, the carrying of mail by air.

Standing near me was a young man who began complaining about being turned away from the McLean House when he tried to see 'Slim' --as he called Lindbergh-- that afternoon. 'But I'll be seeing him in the morning,' he said. 'Lindbergh has invited me and several others who taught him to fly or flew with him to come to the temporary White House at 9 o'clock.' "I introduced myself. The man said he was Frank

CHAPTER 9   THE LINDBERGH CONNECTION

Robertson[1], from St. Louis. A few minutes of conversation revealed that he was an Army aviator who had instructed the fledgling flyer Lindbergh. I said I wished I could join that select number, realizing full well that several million others would like that privilege. I explained that I was teaching journalism and wanted to take this rare opportunity for an interview both as an instructive example and for an article on behalf of the Boy Scouts of America. 'Why not tomorrow?', Robertson queried. 'I'll get you in. Meet me at the north door of the McLean House before nine.'

Frank Robertson

"I was there well before 9 o'clock. Thousands of men, women and children were pressing about the residence and being restrained by police. I edged my way to the entrance. It was guarded by two burly policemen. When Robertson appeared, he simply gave them a card and added: 'This man is invited too. He's with me.'"

"We were ushered into the spacious living room, where eight chairs had been arranged in a semi-circle around a single chair where Lindbergh was to sit. Another chair was brought in for me. Robertson introduced me to the small group as 'a writer from Florida'. Promptly at nine Lindbergh entered the room, smiling bashfully. Instantly all the men

---

[1] Frank Robertson, Cofounder of Robertson Aircraft Corporation, https://en.wikipedia.org/wiki/Robertson_Aircraft_Corporation FAIR USE: Its inclusion in the article adds significantly to the article because the photo and its historical significance are the object of discussion in the article.

sprang to their feet. Their spokesman from St. Louis grasped the hero by the hand. 'Slim!' he said. 'So good to see you.' 'Thank you, Frank. So good of you gentlemen to come!' Lindbergh responded. The celebrity took his seat, and so did his guests, mostly pilots, of which most were mail pilots, and a few were former instructors of Lindbergh.

'Well, Slim, you did it'! said Robertson.

'But you fellows taught me all I know about flying,' Lindbergh countered with a laugh.

'But we didn't teach you how to fly the Atlantic,' the spokesman said. 'Slim, everyone here wants to know what special preparations for the flight did you make after you got to Roosevelt Field (on Long Island)?'

'Well, I did some calculating of my weight. I decided to discard every item that might hold us (the Spirit of St. Louis and me) back. I took no clothes other than my flying suit, not even an extra pair of shoes. I planned to buy an outfit when I arrived in Paris. But by then the American Ambassador, Mr. Herrick, had already done so and presented it to me. I promised to pay him back when I got home, but he said he wouldn't take any money.'

'How about food for that 33 hours, Slim? We hear you did not have a box lunch.'

'No, that would have weighed too much. I took a sandwich or two, wrapped in light paper.'

One of the pilots asked, 'What were your fuel calculations?

'Four hundred gallons to reach Paris. So, I put in 425,' Lindbergh explained in a matter-of-fact voice.

CHAPTER 9   THE LINDBERGH CONNECTION

"Two or three of the men in the room were not pilots. One of them said, 'We understand you did not follow a map.'

'That's right. I flew by dead reckoning.'

'Dead reckoning?' the layman exclaimed. 'You flew the Atlantic by dead reckoning?'

'Yes, I charted the course with a piece of string, which I stretched from Long Island to Paris over a globe, a great circle route. I plotted it in hundreds of miles. There were thirty-six of them. When I had flown a hundred miles, I would turn right by --' he mentioned a certain number of degrees. It was clear that even the flyers present were deeply impressed by Lindbergh's skill at dead reckoning.

Lindbergh continued, 'But nearly halfway across I almost lost my chart. I got so sleepy I opened a window for fresh air, and a gust blew the paper almost out of the plane. I caught it just in time.'

Another asked, 'How did you stay awake all that distance? You hadn't slept for two nights.' 'When I got the report that it was clearing up over the Atlantic, and it was clear at LeBourget Field, I lay down for a few hours, but I did not really sleep. When you have a job to do, as you fellows know, you stay awake to do it.'

"The 'fellows' were silent for several seconds. It was obvious to me what they were thinking. Here was a young pilot, brave enough to risk the Atlantic alone, but also a precise engineer, coldly calculating what his plane would do, how much weight it would carry, how much fuel it would need, how long that Ryan engine would keep on whirling, and what he himself could endure as its lone pilot. After about half an hour Lindbergh thanked the men again for coming to Washington to see him. He stood and Robertson took me by the arm and led me to the guest of honor. 'Slim, this man would like a brief interview for the Boy Scouts of

America.' For the first time, I clasped the hand of the man who became one of my closest friends in later years. Lindbergh sat down, while I drew up a chair. For about ten minutes he answered my questions while men were still milling around, and Lindbergh began chatting with them. I could not help thinking that here was a chance for the White House to show some hospitality.

President Calvin Coolidge awards Lindbergh the Congressional Medal of Honor in 1928

FAIR USE: Its inclusion in the article adds significantly to the article because the photo and its historical significance are the object of discussion in the article.

At least some refreshments, if only punch and cookies, granted that that might have cost the President and First Lady a few dollars. I went into the hall. The curtains over the big windows had been drawn. I pulled them apart enough to peak out at the thousands of people, shouting and waving outside, hoping to land a glimpse of the man they so admired. Suddenly a private elevator opened. One man got out -- President Coolidge. He walked to the window and took a peek at the throng. 'A most enthusiastic crowd, Mr. President', I remarked. 'A great tribute to Charles Lindbergh?' Coolidge dropped the curtain and turned toward me. 'Yes.' That was all he said, and he turned on his heel to disappear down the hall.

CHAPTER 9   THE LINDBERGH CONNECTION

O. K.'s was the only audience the aviator granted a journalist upon his return from Paris. "My brief interview with Lindbergh was published in the Boy Scout Magazine and republished many times. It won for me a request from Boy Scout headquarters that I write a new book of instructions for a Merit Badge: the first one in journalism to be included in the Boy Scout Handbook."

Lindbergh and some friends had attended a show in New York the night before departure. Cloud cover extended the width of the Atlantic and was not expected to clear for some time. After the show, word came that clearing had begun. Lindbergh was in a race and did not want the competition to take advantage. What was left of the night was spent in urgent preparation with a gesture at napping. He was so sleep deprived at takeoff that he had to contend with hallucinations in route.

A retired commercial pilot recalls the psychological impact Lindbergh's flight had on America: "It's hard to conceive without having been there. It transformed everybody's thinking about aviation. But more importantly, it symbolized freedom in the sense that 'We Americans are free to do anything in the world.' It was a spirit of adventure like the Gold Rush days. Private enterprise got serious about building airplanes. Some in the press tried to label Lindbergh as foolhardy, but he was not that at all; he was just very meticulous."

1928 was a busy year for O. K. In addition to teaching eight classes per semester, he wrote his first book, *The Life and Work of Dr. A. A. Murphree*, a biography of the University of Florida's president (in office 1909-1927). He collected material for another book, *Old Massa's People: The Old Slaves Tell Their Story*. He began a textbook on news-writing principles for high school students; wrote an article on Georgia Tech football coach John W. Heisman; collaborated with Melvin Lee, dean of the Columbia University School of Journalism to compile a Boy Scout pamphlet offering vocational guidance to scouts contemplating careers in journalism; and delivered the commencement address for the graduating class at Gainesville's Waldo High School.

Rae O. Weimer, an officer in the administration of the University of Florida while O. K. was there and later dean of the College of Journalism and Communications, characterized O. K. as "a self-starter, innovative and resourceful to developing something original. And he was a hell of a nice guy. If it weren't for him, we wouldn't have had the same kind of support. He was a little ahead of his time." And in a 1983 letter, Journalism School Dean Ralph Lowenstein thanked O. K. for being "the father of journalism education at the University of Florida. Whatever we have become is largely because of the seeds you planted almost 50 years ago . . . Thank you for the role you played in laying solid foundations for the college."

O. K.'s founding of the university's School of Journalism is more significant in the long run but less dramatic than another event of the time. In O. K.'s words, "The late lamented Florida real estate boom was on. There never was a boom like it, and I hope to the Lord there never will be again. We got there just in time to catch it. Everybody was as crazy as bedbugs making money in Florida land. Louise and I had saved a precious few hundred dollars. Here came a fellow saying, 'You need to invest your money in property at Orlando,' then a town of about twelve thousand citizens. I drove our Model T down to have a look. All I had to do was put down $500 on the $2,500 mortgage on lakefront property. My fine comrade of The War, Sergeant John Ross, who had an abundance of money, said, 'Let me know when you decide, O. K., and

CHAPTER 9   THE LINDBERGH CONNECTION

I'll buy in with you.' Ross and I each put down $500 on property on a lake near Orlando. About three weeks later I got a telegram from a realtor asking if I would take $1500 for my part of the property. This illustrates just how deranged people had become. I remember that the news was full of how money was being made, particularly in a certain street in Miami the record had been broken: That property had sold at $40,000 per front foot. It was insane. People would simply quit work, put on silk shirts, knickers and a Panama hat and sell 'binders,' which were options, just paper exchanges. People didn't bother looking at the property. They would just buy and sell the option. They would show the next buyer an abstract of the property's location and make the exchange. Big buses would round up buyers and carry them to Coral Gables, a barren area of streets and twenty-five-foot lots and a huge entrance gate. There they would sell them binders to buy lots. It was a mill. People would buy multiple lots with thoughts of one big home on several lots, or several small homes, but a big profit either way. It was unregulated and wild.

"Under that sort of influence, I turned down the $1,500 offer. Everybody who bought lakefront property wanted to build houses on it, and Ross and I were trying to decide whether to join in. Then came the winter of 1926, and the boom stopped. Historians and economists have analyzed and written about this Florida boom and bust ever since. I don't know what happened, except that it had become entirely out of line with the actual value of the time. In February 1926, some light began to break on reality, and people began to realize they might not get their money back. Investors panicked, tried to unload, and couldn't. Ross was in fine shape and so took over my deed and held it for several years. I think maybe he broke even, but that's questionable. My father by then had become pastor of a church at the little town of Mims, near Titusville.

Two of his deacons, brothers (in genes, not necessarily in Christ), were worth millions in property at the height of the boom. By late February they were penniless. A few survived, simply because they were already using the land, such as for small farms, and did not need to unload regardless of their property's theoretical worth. And many of those were able to sell for handsome profits years later when things regained some sanity. Meanwhile, the bust affected not just Orlando, but the entire state. A professor at the University held the first mortgage on our home in Gainesville and was now insolvent. Creditors were pounding on everybody's door.

CHAPTER 10

THE LURE OF THE OZARKS

In July of '27, O. K. Jr. ("Kay") was born at Gainesville's only medical facility most resembling a hospital, the University of Florida Infirmary. By May of 1928 the School of Journalism was strong enough to make a go of it, so in typical Armstrong fashion, O. K. said to Louise, "Let's get away from this madness. Let's move back to Missouri." "Louise and I packed our worldly possessions and our two-year old infant son into our Model T for the two-week trip to Missouri".

Kay Armstrong 1928

In 1992, Anadarcia Sirianni, a University of Florida graduate student, completed her master's thesis titled "Orland Kay Armstrong: Writer, Educator, and Public Servant. A Thesis Presented to the Graduate Council of the University of Florida in Partial Fulfillment of the Requirements for the Degree of Master of Arts in Mass Communications." Her abstract begins: "With the encouragement of University of Florida President Dr. A. A. Murphree, Orland Kay Armstrong, a recent journalism master graduate, launched the journalism department at the University of Florida. The results of this study indicated that Armstrong was a spokesman for the rights of the underdog

CHAPTER 10   THE LURE OF THE OZARKS

and for equality for all through his lifestyle of integrity and honesty." Chapter One begins: "A prominent Orlando attorney (J. Thomas Gurney) who knew Orland Kay Armstrong for more than half a century, once described him as 'an unusually talented writer of high moral sense who was devoted to the American principle of government and honor, a pleasant and entertaining companion and, above all, a gentleman of the first order."

Ms. Sirianni continues, "Armstrong was responsible for articles that helped chronicle history and intriguing events, but no one has taken a comprehensive look at this crusading Scots-Irishman. Even if it meant a sacrifice of income, if there was a purpose or direction that he thought was worthy and urgent, he would devote himself to it. Armstrong had a vision of a peace-filled future and a willingness to lead the people toward that future. He used his writing and political activism to warn people of the consequences of not meeting a particular problem or to call them to an opportunity that was being missed."

O. K., looking back upon their return to Springfield, "If I had had the sense of a goose, I would have filed for Congress in 1928. I could have had the nomination because the man from Sedalia who finally announced was reluctant and on the outs with the party anyway."

CHAPTER 11

FREELANCE JOURNALIST

Instead of seizing the day politically--his first of three watershed failures to do so--O. K. launched a career as a magazine writer. Freelance journalism was a hard living, but a living. He wrote for the Saturday Evening Post, Country Gentlemen, Colliers, The American Legion, This Week, Nation's Business, Saturday Evening Post, Harpers, Christian Herald, and many others. He had only just heard about the Readers Digest. His first published article, about the American Legion Hospital for Crippled Children in St. Petersburg Florida, appeared in the November 1929 issue of American Legion Magazine.

O. K.' s second book, published in 1931, was *Old Massa's People: The Old Slaves Tell Their Story*. The Dedication reads, "To My Wife, Louise McCool Armstrong, Fair Granddaughter of the Old South, I affectionately Inscribe This Story of Slavery Days." O. K. spent years researching this portrayal of the culture of old Dixie by interviewing, in every state of the Confederacy, more than twelve hundred former slaves in their ninth to eleventh decades of life. "Armstrong was skilled as an interviewer, making his subjects feel at ease. He was at home with any group without regard to its members' profession or to their current or ancestral culture. The purpose of the book was to depict the Old South as the Negro saw it. The book compiles the stories of those brought into the sphere of cruel traders and owners and of those more fortunate, of whom Mammy in *Gone with the Wind* is a reminder, brought into the inner sanctum of the owner's family. He wrote it in their vernacular and did so

CHAPTER 11 FREELANCE JOURNALIST

with a respect which bespoke a fondness of, even a kinship with, those he interviewed, which wasn't surprising in as much as he knew a thing or two about humble circumstances. He wrote in the margin of his 1930 notes for the book: "What they need: 1) Justice; 2) Education; 3) Special industrial training --Make the Negro an asset."

O. K. Armstrong was an early proponent of civil rights for African-Americans and Native Americans. Today, political forces have distorted the truth about the plight of black slaves in the South. The agrarian economy of the South was pre-industrial and slavery was the unfortunate result. There was racial abuse in the South and in the North, that is uncontested, but that was not the norm according to the black slaves themselves. Their story is presented in their own words in Armstrong's *OLD MASSA'S PEOPLE*. Recent events have overtaken the truth in this matter and there are evil forces using the history of slavery in America to drive a wedge between various factions in order to implement a Marxist form of government. Statues of Civil War heroes on both sides of the issue are being toppled by mindless mobs that are being incited by anarchists and Marxists. While it is clear that those in the Confederacy were traitors to the Union, many were protecting what they thought to be their homeland. This was a decision that General Robert E. Lee made as a Virginian. It was the wrong decision, but the matter was settled with the defeat of the South. The true hero of the time was President Abraham Lincoln who recognized that the Nation would need to heal. Today, anarchists and Marxists are toppling the statutes of Lee and other symbols of the Confederacy, but they are also toppling and defacing statues of Abraham Lincoln, Ulysses S. Grant and even great abolitionists. The mindless mob will never read *OLD MASSA'S PEOPLE*, and that is unfortunate.

CHAPTER 12

THE DREAM HOUSE

In the Introduction to her thesis, Ms. Sirianni wrote: "O. K.'s heritage built into him a generous and optimistic spirit, which was matched by Louise's. He was forever willing to share what he had, and on many occasions through the years of his life he would provide housing, education and sustenance to relatives." By late 1932, Louise's brother-in law, married to her sister Bernice, had lost his job as a tobacco auctioneer in Raleigh, and thereby became still another victim of the Great Depression. O. K and Louise invited them to come to Springfield and share their small, two-bedroom, one-bath house with them and the two small boys.

Mom Louise with Kay and Milton

In February 1933, "Little Sister" was born, and they named her for her mother, Louise. The "Little Sister" designation was necessary since in the southern tradition, her mother Louise was called Sister and her older brother was called Brother by her family. With two couples and three youngsters, the house was becoming crowded. Early in 1934, O. K. drove his car around the streets of Springfield, searching for a larger but affordable house. He noticed a huge, vacant house with the front door

CHAPTER 12 THE DREAM HOUSE

standing open. He walked into the house and admired the woodwork, the spaciousness and the seven ornate fireplaces. The twelve-foot-wide hallway was paneled in walnut, front to back, which extended up the massive stairway and throughout the upstairs hallway. The dining room was paneled in butternut or, perhaps, cherry, and had a bay window overlooking the broad lawn with thirteen oak trees. Each of the four big bedrooms upstairs was trimmed in a different wood: oak, cherry, mahogany and elm.

When O. K. walked out, the gentleman next door, Ed V. Williams, a department store owner comfortably surviving the depression, rushed over to greet him.

"O. K., would you like to buy this house? Over ten thousand square feet-plus basement, 50-foot-wide attic and 1870s servants' area. The Sigma Nu's couldn't keep up the payments and moved to the dorms even after I lowered the rent."

"Ed, I don't have the money to buy a house like this."

"I'll rent it to you for $35 per month."

1307 Benton Avenue, Springfield, Missouri

"Well, it's more house than we need, but maybe we can get our money out of it if I can turn the servants' quarters into an apartment." O. K. and Louise were renting the house for $35 when Mr. Williams died. Williams's lawyer called. "O. K., we've got to do something with that house you're in. We have got to sell it. I've been authorized to sell it to you for $5,000 plus four hundred for our agent if you can come up with a hundred down." It took O. K. twelve years to pay it off.

O. K. Armstrong and son O. K. Armstrong Jr. (Kay)

Many years later (1963) the property would be acquired by Lester Cox as an expansion of the Burge-Protestant Hospital of Springfield which would later become Cox-North Hospital. The Armstrong property was converted to a parking lot. As part of the real estate transaction, the home's original construction material would be owned by the Armstrong's. Stanley Armstrong would be assigned the responsibility for the project. The old home was dismantled piece by piece and shipped to the area of the Wilson's Creek Battlefield near

CHAPTER 12 — THE DREAM HOUSE

Republic, Missouri, southwest of the city of Springfield. There the material would be used to construct the family's new residence.

The family would painstakingly move the more exquisite architectural components such as the walnut fireplace, wainscot, and staircase to the new home. The new home would be called "The Highlands." It was built to resemble George Washington's Mount Vernon Home.

According to Kay Armstrong, "In my dad's original Will he had wanted the property to remain in the family and to belong to any of his children who desired to keep it. However, this Will was replaced by a trust that O. K. and Marjorie arranged before my dad passed away. After living alone for a few years, Marjorie decided to sell the property and was assisted by her brother Lieutenant General Joseph Harold Moore in making the arrangements. Unfortunately, as a retired Air Force officer, General Moore was not familiar with the property values in the Springfield area at the time and convinced Marjorie to sell the property which consisted of the home and 20 acres(two 10-acre tracts) to Dr. Thomas P. Sweeney for $187,000.

Dr. Sweeney had moved with his family to Springfield in the late 1960s to join the Springfield Radiological Group. He was an avid historian and a member of the Civil War Round Table of the Ozarks, the Greene County Historical Society, and Wilson's Creek National Battlefield Foundation. Dr. Sweeney created the General Sweeney museum in the early 1990s, naming it after his ancestor, General Thomas Sweeney who fought in the Mexican and Civil Wars. He had collected artifacts of the Civil War from all over the U. S. and displayed them in the museum. The artifacts, the home and its 20 acres were later appraised together as a bundle for over $ 4 million. The actual breakdown in values is unknown but the bundle of artifacts and property were acquired by the National Park Service in 2005 through a Federal grant sponsored by then U. S. Congressman Roy Blunt." The home was later used as an office for the Wilson's Creek Battlefield historical site and museum for a while. The home still stands at 5176 South State Highway ZZ on the way to Republic, Missouri. Dr. Sweeney died on December 9, 2019 after a long battle with Alzheimer's.

The "HIGHLANDS"

CHAPTER 13

THE GREAT DEPRESSION

Charles Armstrong's research into the Armstrong family was very thorough. The following is an example. "Those of us who did not experience the Great Depression but want to envision it must put to the unaided eye a lens that will fix on a world not our own. A few other signs of the times might help: O.K.'s sister Delta began teaching high school in Lake Butler, Florida, not long after her family settled there in 1919. In 1930, she was notified by the Lake Butler school district that all teachers would be paid with 'warrants,' promises to pay when cash was available. Sometimes cash became available, sometimes it didn't. In 1932, their brother Noble, with his PhD in education from Duke, got a job teaching Education at Columbus (Mississippi) College for Women, the nation's oldest state supported college for women, for $60 per month plus board in the dining hall.

Crooked River Club

During the late 1920s, Louise's brother Dennard McCool established the Crooked River Club, a lodge for 'sportsmen' wanting to take advantage of Nature's bounty in the river and the surrounding marshes and forest. The club was

CHAPTER 13   THE GREAT DEPRESSION

near the town of St. Mary in southeast Georgia. It was a lush setting, semi-tropical and sensuous, the evening breeze carrying in the smells and warm weather sounds of the river and swamp. He went into sizeable debt to build the big $20,000 inn.

End of the Hunt

During the mid-thirties, their profit margin narrowed to the point of failure. When they raised the price of their nightly seafood banquet from 50 cents to 65, they took a barrage of complaints from their patrons, mainly professional people and those whose inherited wealth survived the 1929 crash--the only folk who could entertain thoughts of recreational travel."

While back in Missouri In November 1932, O. K. was elected to the state legislature and re-elected in 1934. A letter to the editor of the Springfield News-Leader by one A.C. Hayward after the 1932 election read as follows:

"To say I am glad Greene County kept enough head to send to the legislature that brilliant young chap, Orland K. Armstrong, is putting it mildly. O. K. is a brother Ozarkian-Hillcrofter of mine. He is a writer, a statesman and an orator of the first water" (a favorite superlative of the day). "His Old Massa's People is one of the great regional books of the hour. He is one of the coming sons of this grand old state. Aside from these marks, he is about the most human, lovable character you ever knew."

In April 1933, O. K. received a letter from a former colleague, Elmer Emig, Professor of Journalism at the University of Florida. After describing changes that had occurred on the campus and throughout Gainesville since 1928, Professor Emig ends with: "O. K., your slavery book was a good one, and well done. I hear reactions to the prison-camp article in the *Herald-Tribune*. Keep up the good work. How does it look for Congress? I hope things will shift the opportunity to you; You deserve it, and you can handle it with glory." But by the mid '30s, times were too lean for divided labor, so O. K. dropped elective politics to focus on writing.

According to Charles, "A bit more Depression lore is O. K.'s outreach to the freight-train hobos. He let it be known that he would provide them with meals and pay for work. They would jump off the boxcars at the Frisco station and go to certain homes that had 'codes,' penciled notices posted on front doors of homes to let the hobos know whether or not they were welcome and what they would get for work. O. K. would let them paint or rake leaves for a meal and maybe a dollar, which would buy enough food for a couple of days. He also tried to motivate them to reform their bad habits and learn a skill."

In 1935 Harry Truman entered the U.S. Senate. In 1941, he was named chairman of a committee serving as watchdog over the treasury. Believing Truman's work deserved recognition, O. K. wrote an article for the *Saturday Evening Post* titled "Billion Dollar Watchdog." The article made a big impression on the media, hence on the citizenry. It brought Truman to the attention of President Roosevelt, and O. K. to that of

CHAPTER 13   THE GREAT DEPRESSION

Dewitt Wallace, founder of the *Reader's Digest*. After reading "Billion Dollar Watchdog," Mr. Wallace invited O. K. to join his small staff of permanent writers (most *Reader's Digest* articles were condensed from other sources; Only one or two per issue were by The Digest's own). For O. K. it meant finding in Wallace one of his life's closest friends, and no more free-lance frazzle.

Government, world and American history, and politics were the dominant themes of O. K.'s more than 120 articles for the Digest; Other themes were the scope of human experience. For example, his first story for Wallace was titled "Barriers Between the States Must Go!" about interstate trade taxes. The sight of that first *Reader's Digest* paycheck brought Louise to tears, primarily for the recognition it meant for her husband. But there would be other recognition that would not be as pleasant.

Charles would relate, "When home, O. K.'s time was the kids' for every needed father thing, but he tried to make every other minute productive. Favored descriptions of such behavior include 'disciplined,' 'compulsive,' 'workaholic,' 'dedicated,' and 'broke.' For O. K., the kids would say it was more of the last two, since 'dedicated' really means 'love of job.' He would write at home and at the interview site, of course. But he would write on the card table at the back of a train coach and on the lunch tray of an airplane. He would burn a pound's worth of candle tallow staying up to get the job done."

While on "vacation" at Uncle Dennard's sportsman's paradise on the banks of Crooked River in south Georgia, he wrote in the boat on a briefcase on the keelson board next to the tackle box. In the evening he would write by kerosene lantern at Uncle Dennard's clubhouse, a pleasant setting for Work. If at a clan gathering on the Florida coast, he would write on the beach under the shade. Even his daily exercise had to be productive--building a shed or a wall or chopping wood.

In September 1940, O. K. and Louise invited their nephew Dennard McCool, son of Louise's big brother, to come live with them and attend high school with Milton and Kay. Southern Georgia at the time provided only ten grades of school. In late 1941, a news bulletin interrupted one of Dennard's favorite radio programs. He bolted into O. K.'s study and exclaimed, "The Japanese have attacked Pearl Harbor!" Much later, O. K. looked back: "Before that, FDR was spouting his fibs, for example, during one of his radio talks he said, 'I pledge to you parents that your boys will never have to go into any foreign war'. I called downstairs, 'Louise, did you hear that? I'll make a prediction: Before these boys are grown, they'll all be in uniform.'" And he was right.

Milton, Charles, Louise, Stanley and Kay (Milton headed for Navy Flight School)

Milton Armstrong 1942

CHAPTER 13   THE GREAT DEPRESSION

The Lindbergh-Armstrong friendship continued after the war. Lindbergh was supportive of Armstrong's political endeavors in Missouri. Armstrong was elected to the Missouri state legislature for several terms, but District gerrymandering would prevent another run for the Missouri legislature. He also made an unsuccessful bid to be the Lieutenant Governor of Missouri.

Lindbergh's support, along with Armstrong's own considerable skills, may have helped Armstrong get elected to serve one term in the U.S. House of Representatives for Missouri from January 1951 to January 1953. But, until then, his passion was in writing.

Kay Armstrong in 1945

Congressman O.K. Armstrong

CHAPTER 14

CRUSADER FOR JUSTICE

O. K. Armstrong's interviews and writing reached freed former slaves to main-event figures, including Herbert Hoover, Richard Nixon, Republic of China President Chiang Kai-shek, Admiral Richard E. Byrd, Orville Wright, Louisiana Governor Huey P. Long, John D. Rockefeller, and non-politicals such as football coach John W. Heisman. As Darci Sirianni points out on page two of her thesis, whoever faced him, whether interviewee or public audience, was at ease regardless of origin, station, accent or education.

The articles he wrote about the American Indians, a series during the 1940s and another during the '50s, are typical of his use of the pen as a crusader's lance. The following paragraph is an excerpt from his 1945 article "Set the American Indians Free!"

"Few know the shameful story of the present status of the Indians. Although all native Indians were declared citizens of the United States by act of Congress in 1924, the act made no provision for the details of their emancipation. In three important respects, they have never been emancipated: They are restricted in property rights. They live under conditions of racial segregation. And they are subject to special limitations and exemptions because they are Indians. Despite government outlays, most reservation Indians live in poverty. Until war work came, not more than two percent of reservation families averaged more than $500 income per year. Disease is prevalent and infant mortality is high. Edwin Stanton, Lincoln's Secretary of War, said, 'The government never reforms an evil until the people demand it.' When this reaches the heart of the American people, the Indians will be saved."

In his 1948 article, "Let's Give the Indians Back to the Country," O. K. proposed a five-point plan: 1) Congress should close the Office of Indian Affairs; 2) Abandon federal control of Indian reservations; 3) Grant Indians all rights of citizenship; 4) Transfer Indian education to the states, and 5) Assist Indians to become self-supporting. In an address to Congress O. K. said: "Certainly those Indians who want to retain their ancient culture and ways of life should be permitted to do so, but they can do that without the supervision of a Federal Bureau."[2]

According to Charles, there was "at least one article by O. K. on a lighter subject. In 1955 the Digest published his story, "The Funniest Football Game Ever Played." In 1922, Georgia Tech dispatched Cumberland University two hundred twenty-two to nothing. Cumberland fielded a "rag-tag, bob-tail" team of eleven men. Neither team made a first down during the game. Cumberland's best play was a three-yard loss. At halftime, with the score 115-0, Tech coach John Heisman said to his players, "Now be careful boys, be on the alert. We don't know what they've got up their sleeve." After the game, Heisman kept his men on the field for a scrimmage workout so they wouldn't miss a day of practice.

In his later years, the Press would be a bit kinder to O. K. The Springfield News & Leader would take a step back from its headlong rush to the left in politics and publish an article that gave a bit of a more favorable review of its famous Republican Congressman and journalist than in its previous coverage of the now elder statesman. In 1984 Don

---

[2] Congressional Record 4378

Mahnken, a writer for the Springfield News & Leader wrote a piece entitled "Interned doctor recalls help of Armstrong" The article was based on an interview with Dr. Y. Fred Fujikawa, a chest surgeon who was semi-retired in Seal Beach, California. He was speaking of the early years of World War II, when Japanese-Americans found themselves interned as a security measure after the attack on Pearl Harbor on December 7, 1941. The feelings did not die quickly. The following is a re-transcription of the article:

> "It was March 30, 1944, when a member of the Missouri House of Representatives from Atchison County offered an amendment which he said 'would prevent wholesale importation and employment of Japanese in our hospitals.' The target was Dr. Fujikawa, whose father and mother came to the United States in 1900 and 1905. Fujikawa was born in America on July 4, 1910. Fujikawa was a 1934 graduate of Creighton University School of Medicine in Missouri and was practicing in Los Angeles at the time of the attack on Pearl Harbor. He found himself languishing in an internment camp at Jerome, Arkansas in 1943. He was paid $19 a month to treat fellow Japanese-American internees. When an opening at the Missouri State Sanatorium in Mount Vernon was posted at the camp, Fujikawa sought and was granted permission to apply. He was accepted and began a six-year stay as a chest surgeon in November 1943.
>
> It was his employment that Representative J. A. Gray attacked. Before the Gray amendment could be ruled out of order --- an action that came later—Representative O. K. Armstrong took the floor. "If we prevent a man from pursuing his honorable profession because his ancestors were Oriental, we would be fanning coals of racial prejudice that might burs into raging flames,'. O. K. began. "Already we are distressed by outcroppings of interracial friction. Already we

CHAPTER 14 CRUSADER FOR JUSTICE

hear it said, "When this is over, we'll put the Negro back in his place." "Let us not punish the innocent victims of war for the crimes of those who are the enemies of freedom . . . Let us then deny the implication that white Americans are the super race. Grateful as I am for my heritage, I cannot take credit for being born a white man. That was God's will. And if I were a Japanese, or the son of any other race, and could be born in this land of liberty, I would thank God that I am an American citizen."

In the following month, the News & Leader published letters that were harshly critical of the appointment of Fujikawa to the sanatorium staff, which promoted a number of letters defending the doctor and his employment.

At first there was some opposition, 'said Ermadean Moored, Mount Vernon a retired registered nurse who worked with Fujikawa's at the chest hospital."

As soon as people knew them, they accepted them and loved them. It was a difficult time. Those people were American citizens. It was so terrible they were picked up out of their homes and put in relocation centers.'

Memories of the incident were revived recently when Fujikawa and his wife Alice, in route to the 50th reunion of the Creighton graduating class on the Armstrong's at their southwest Greene County home. 'I was never more impressed with my husband's eloquence and dignity than when I saw these two in tears because of my husband's defense of his right and the hospital's right,' said Marjorie Armstrong.

Explained Fujikawa: 'I just want to shake Mr. Armstrong's hand. He was so instrumental in changing my life.'

The had met before, Fujikawa recalled the time in '1946 or so' when Armstrong was driving by the Fujikawa home in Mount Vernon, stopped and introduced himself.

The events of 1943-44 resulted in a change of direction for the doctor. 'I was in general practice when I came to the Missouri State Sanatorium, Fujikawa said. 'That was my training in chest. I left as a tuberculosis surgeon.'

Armstrong's stand in the Missouri House and a subsequent action by the Speaker of the House also ensured Fujikawa's future away from the internment camps.

The confinement was real, the doctor said. 'There were guard towers, soldiers and machine guns. They were for our protection they said, but the guns were pointing inward. We were told it was dangerous outside. And there were incidents where a Japanese-American soldier in uniform being shot in one of the towns when he came down to visit his family in the camp.'

Fujikawa specialized in thoracic surgery and tuberculosis when he returned to California in January 1949. However, four coronaries and arthritis in his hands stopped his surgical practice in 1975. The Fujikawa's have three children, the oldest son born in the Arkansas camp and now a physician specializing in neurology. A daughter is a clinical psychologist, married to a physician. The youngest son is a lawyer.

Of the visit with the Armstrong's, Fujikawa said, 'It was the high point of my trip.'

He left a note on the guest book of the Armstrong's: 'I cannot thank you enough, you kindness and support during those trying day in 1944, when I was at the Missouri State Sanatorium in Mount Vernon and you alone stood up for me in the state legislature.' Armstrong explained his position. 'All I know is, I always have been for the underdog.'"

CHAPTER 15

CRUSADER FOR PEACE

Charles Armstrong felt that, "I believe I can speak with some authority on my father's ideology of war and peace. It includes these principles: The good must remain stronger than the aggressor. Peace is not just the absence of war, but it must be built into the character and lives of our many leaders and few statesmen."

His canon was that peace is predicated upon freedom and international justice. After the Great War, he became increasingly concerned about the spread of totalitarianism--National Socialism (Nazism), Communism and Fascism. And although his theology might not have been rated orthodox by all (but whose is?), he believed that Christianity's emphasis on the sanctity of the individual–as opposed to any collective power--provided the moral force by which the Western world civilized its culture and protects its citizens from tyranny. He believed that the principles of freedom and justice that evolved through Western Civilization, the Christian moral compass, was the ultimate answer to totalitarianism and aggression.

Before December 7, 1941, O. K. had vigorously protested the U.S. blockade of Japan's oil imports, warning that it would provoke war. As for the war in Europe, O. K. and Charles Lindbergh teamed up to oppose an early American entry. To them, allying with one totalitarian power over another was arbitrary, short-sighted and counterproductive, a mistimed involvement of America. In short, an alliance with a totalitarian power was an alliance with iniquity. They believed it wiser to let Hitler

CHAPTER 15   CRUSADER FOR PEACE

and Stalin, whose regimes were the two greatest evils of the middle-aged century, go at each other, after which the U.S. would pick up the pieces militarily and politically and construct a stable peace free of totalitarianism. O. K.'s thinking was that Stalin and Hitler would likely fight to a draw. Then the United States could step in and provide leadership with the peace and reconstruction. If, on the other hand, one totalitarian regime should begin to gain the upper hand over the other, then America could intervene and quickly prevail over a debilitated foe.

The following order of events were chronicled in ANNALS OF IOWA, *Courtesy of De Moines Register and Tribune*. The following is a synopsis of the article titled "Verne Marshall in 1940":

"On December 17, 1940, at New York's Hotel Lexington, Verne Marshall, editor of the *Cedar Rapids Gazette*, announced the formation of the No Foreign War Committee. Like most other isolationists, Marshall felt that the United States should build an impregnable defense. While at times Lindbergh wanted isolationists throughout the nation to buck the America First Committee, at other times he thought that two regional associations might operate more effectively. Lindbergh reluctantly endorsed the appointment of Verne Marshall as chairman. Within two days after the organization of the No Foreign War Committee was announced, Marshall noted that Lindbergh had promised to "do everything this committee wants me to do." Plans were made for a mass meeting in St. Louis, where the official campaign would be launched.

Pacifists were scheduled to play an important role in the new organization. O. K. Armstrong called an Emergency Peace Conference in Washington on October 21, 1940, with his old friend, Colonel Lindbergh, as the featured speaker. Pacifists were there in abundance at the conference. Later, in a letter written to R. Douglas Stuart, national director of America First, Lindbergh admitted that he differed with the pacifists on what he called "strong military forces for American Defense," but claimed that "the agitation for war and the trend towards it in this country have been so strong that I don't think we can afford to alienate any groups who stand with us in opposition." [A take on "the enemy of my enemy is my friend".] Therefore, with his belief that all antiwar forces must coordinate their efforts, Lindbergh wanted Armstrong to merge his No Foreign War Campaign with Verne Marshall's No Foreign War Committee. But, to maintain some control, he pressed for Armstrong to direct the field organization of Marshall's new group.

At first, efforts to gain pacifist backing seemed successful. But within two months after its birth on December 17, 1940, the No Foreign War Committee ceased major political activity ,and four months later it formally disbanded. Charles A. Lindberg withdrew his support, and O. K. Armstrong also withdrew support from the Committee.

At a supper at Lindbergh's home on January 4, 1941, Armstrong and the Lone Eagle discussed the possibility of forming still another antiwar group, one which would sponsor mass meetings throughout the country. After a trip to New York in a last-ditch effort to wrest control of the Committee from Marshall, Armstrong submitted his resignation. The death of the No Foreign War Committee had few mourners. Most of its backers were strongly opposed to the domestic reforms of the previous ten years and found even the America First Committee--by no means a radical group--far too liberal." Although many Americans opposed Roosevelt's interventionism, this would all change on December 7, 1941.

CHAPTER 15　　CRUSADER FOR PEACE

O. K. enlisted Charles Lindbergh's help, hoping Lindbergh's prestige would be influential. A letter from O. K. to Louise, June 6, 1940, letterhead: Hotel Astor (not the Waldorf-Astoria) Times Square, NY, reads: "My Lover, it is eleven o'clock. I have just left Lindbergh. We were nearly four hours talking. His heart and soul wrapped up in my plans. He said he would help--would raise money, speak, do anything to keep this country out of war. I really enjoyed him. I showed him the pictures. He got a laugh out of little Stanley trotting along the walk. I'd phone you if it didn't cost so much."

O. K. remembered: "I was up to my neck in the keep-out-of-war campaign. We knew Roosevelt desperately wanted to get us into war. We knew he would if he could, and he could, and he did." In early October 1941, the Japanese embassy's top attorney [there's a special word for it], knowing of Lindbergh and Armstrong's effort, called O. K. from Washington to request a meeting. In O.K.'s words: "I went to his hotel. He sat on his bed, and if you ever saw the face of dejection, this was it. I said, 'Mr. Terasake, what has happened?'

'Something terrible, Mr. Armstrong. Prince Konoye and the Peace Party in Japan have fallen. Admiral Tojo, the new Premier, is in total charge of my country and is a war hawk bent on breaking through Mr. Roosevelt's oil embargo. This will undoubtedly mean war'.

The politics of it was that FDR knew the Japanese would make war on us if we cut off the oil. Roosevelt could have supplied it, but he convinced the British, the Dutch, and so on, to join an embargo, knowing this would go far and probably all the way to incite war. Later we learned that FDR had tried to get Hitler to attack by sinking some of his submarines, which he ordered our Navy to do during 1940 and 1941. Hitler knew what that meant and wouldn't take the bait."

Integral to this history is the Kimmel-Short affair. After the Pearl Harbor disaster, civilian leaders in Washington needed cover. Rear Admiral Husband Kimmel and Maj. General Walter Short, the ranking officers at Pearl Harbor on the Sunday morning of December 7, 1941 -- the Day of Infamy -- were blamed for the success of the Japanese assault. Shortly after the U.S. declaration of war, Kimmel and Short were accused of being derelict in their duties and were relieved of their commands. Their request for courts- martial [with which] to clear their names was never granted. Upward of a dozen hearings, investigations and conferences were held on this issue over half a century. Dereliction of duty charges were repudiated by these investigations. The two top naval combat commanders in the Pacific Theater during World War II were Admirals William F. Halsey and Raymond A. Spruance.

Admiral Halsey wrote: "In all my experience, I have never known a commander-in-chief of any United States fleet who worked harder, and under more adverse circumstances, to increase its efficiency and to prepare for war; Furthermore, I know of no officer who might have been in command at that time who could have done more than Admiral Kimmel did."

Admiral Spruance wrote: "I have always felt that Kimmel and Short were held responsible for Pearl Harbor in order that the American people might have no reason to lose confidence in their government in Washington." Defense Under Secretary Edwin Dorn's report, subsequent to the Senate's final (1995) investigation, disclosed officially that blame should be "broadly shared." Dorn's report confirmed that members of the high command in Washington were privy to intercepted Japanese messages that in their totality . . . pointed strongly toward an

CHAPTER 15   CRUSADER FOR PEACE

attack on Pearl Harbor on the 7th of December 1941, and that the intelligence was never sent to the commanders in Hawaii. Vice Admiral David C. Richardson criticized the Dorn report for not specifying those who should "share the blame."

In January 1941, our ambassador to Japan had reported that in the case of a break with the United States, the Japanese were planning "a surprise mass attack on Pearl Harbor." In July 1941, the chief of the Navy War Plans Division named Hawaii as the probable target of a Japanese air assault. At the same time, Navy Secretary Frank Knox wrote to Secretary of War Henry Stimson, "Hostilities would be initiated by a surprise attack on Pearl Harbor." By August 1940, American cryptographers had deciphered the Japanese diplomatic code. On Nov. 22, 1941, they intercepted a message from the Japanese government to their envoys negotiating with the Roosevelt administration, notifying them that in about a week "things are automatically going to happen." A few days before the aerial raid the FBI reported that the Japanese consulate in Honolulu was burning its diplomatic papers. In spite of these warnings, there were no special guards on any of the ships at Pearl. The fleet was on its loosest alert. Only 25 percent of its anti-aircraft guns were manned, and half the officers were on shore leave. As a cost-cutting measure, weekend reconnaissance flights were canceled. At the airfields, planes were lined up wingtip to wingtip, making them perfect targets for aerial bombing. The setting at Oahu was ideal for Captain Mitsuo Fuchida's Nakajima-97 bombers, Aichi dive bombers and Zeroes –142 planes in all.

An article in the May/June reissue of "Naval History," the magazine of the United States Naval Institute titled "Advance Warning? The Red Cross Connection" by Daryl S. Borgquist presents evidence that

President Roosevelt ordered a secret shipment of surgical supplies to the Red Cross in Hawaii in anticipation of the attack on Pearl Harbor. The article is persuasive that Mr. Roosevelt summoned Don C. Smith, director of the War Service for the Red Cross, to his office to inform Smith of the news of which the President's intelligence staff had informed him, that an attack on Pearl harbor by the Japanese was pending, that supplies should be sent to a port-of-entry on the west coast, and that no one, including military and Red Cross personnel in Hawaii, was to be informed. Roosevelt countered Smith's protests with a description of the Presidential motive: The American people would never agree to enter war short of an attack on U.S. territory.

O. K. continues: "Lindbergh and I were convinced that without U.S. intervention the Nazis and the Allies would come to a draw, at which time we could step in and make sure that the whole lot of totalitarianism was swept away, and with minimal loss of American lives. Hitler's thrust was to the east: Drang nach Osten. He was afraid of drawing America in. After his aggression in Czechoslovakia I think he would have stopped at a line short of drawing in the British. Hitler wanted to make peace with England partly because of his perception of German-English kinship as Nordic races, partly to get England's help to defeat Russia. Dunkerque closed that door. If the Japanese had had the oil they wanted, they would have settled their hostilities with China, and I think they would have been neutral toward the United States.

"The first week of November, E. Stanley Jones, an influential missionary and pacifist who was close to Mr. Roosevelt, phoned me to ask if he could join our effort. [Stanley Armstrong was named after E. Stanley Jones] I arranged a meeting to include Mr. Terasake, Mr. Jones

CHAPTER 15 CRUSADER FOR PEACE

and me. Mr. Terasake was terribly agitated with the possibility that his government was preparing an assault. So, I went to the Japanese embassy as soon as I could schedule a meeting with Admiral Nomura, the special ambassador sent in just before Pearl Harbor. On November 30, I told him I would do everything I could to prevent war between our countries. The ambassador shook his head and said, 'I'm afraid it's too late.' He either already knew of the plan or suspected the carriers were due to sail within days to blast Pearl Harbor if they could.

"Seven days after the blitz, on December 14, while in Washington doing research, I went by Mr. Terasake's apartment. He was not there. He had been interned. He had been separated from his American wife and their six- year-old daughter. I slipped by the secret service men guarding the apartment. Inside, I asked Mrs. Terasake: 'Was my correspondence saved?' 'No, every bit of paper was burned.' All Japanese diplomats were herded down to White Sulfur Springs, Virginia."

From the modest lectern of a state legislator, O. K. vigorously denounced the post-Pearl Harbor internment of Japanese Americans as a cynical propaganda maneuver designed to stir war hysteria. "The Japanese-Americans had been here for decades or even generations. They were industrious, and they were as good Americans as those who said, 'off with their heads.' The state with the most Japanese was California. Governor Earl Warren should have stopped the incarceration but didn't--that's how great the pressure was. During wartime, the pressure is difficult to resist. But that didn't rob some of us of our calm sense. I knew what was going on.' I promptly got a call from the (Springfield) News-Leader: 'O. K., what do think about this Pearl Harbor situation?'

I replied, 'Well, it means we're at war, and we'll have to win it. But I'm convinced the Japanese people knew nothing about Pearl Harbor, and I'm also convinced the Japanese people did not want war with America.' Pretty soon some of the hotheads in our American Legion post had a meeting at Judge Fairman's office at the Landers building in Springfield to debate what to do about O. K. Armstrong, who 'has spoken treason.' Since 1929 I had been in charge of the Legion's child-welfare program and a member since shortly after World War I. They said, 'Well, let's just return his dues and expel him from our post.' That hit the newspaper. Immediately I had calls from three other posts asking me to join."

CHAPTER 15   CRUSADER FOR PEACE

Most people are familiar with the remarkable story of the brave "Lucky Lindy" and his solo flight across the Atlantic. And many know the tragic story of the kidnapping of his young son. But the friendship between O. K. Armstrong and Lindbergh is glossed over in the annals of History. Here we have to back up a bit in this History to accurately reflect the role of Lindbergh in the build-up to the War and the War itself. Their friendship develops just before the United States entered the Second World War. The background is as follows:

Charles Augustus Lindbergh

"At the urging of U.S. Ambassador Joseph Kennedy, Lindbergh wrote a secret memo to the British warning that a military response by Britain and France to Hitler's violation of the Munich Agreement would be disastrous; he claimed that France was militarily weak and Britain over-reliant on its navy. He recommended that they urgently strengthen their air power to force Hitler to redirect his aggression against 'Asiatic Communism'. In a controversial 1939 Reader's Digest article he wrote, 'Our civilization depends on peace among Western nations ... and therefore on united strength, for Peace is a virgin who dare not show her face without Strength, her father, for protection.'[3] Lindbergh deplored the rivalry

---

[3] https://en.wikipedia.org/wiki/Charles_Lindbergh

between Germany and Britain but favored a war between Germany and Russia.

Following Hitler's invasion of Czechoslovakia and Poland, Lindbergh decried suggestions that the United States should send aid to countries under threat, writing, 'I do not believe that repealing the arms embargo would assist democracy in Europe' and, 'If we repeal the arms embargo with the idea of assisting one of the warring sides to overcome the other, then why mislead ourselves by talk of neutrality?' He equated assistance with war profiteering: 'To those who argue that we could make a profit and build up our own industry by selling munitions abroad, I reply that we in America have not yet reached a point where we wish to capitalize on the destruction and death of war.'

In his 1941 testimony before the House Committee on Foreign Affairs opposing the Lend-Lease bill, Lindbergh proposed that the United States negotiate a neutrality pact with Germany. President Franklin Roosevelt publicly decried Lindbergh's views as those of a 'defeatist and appeaser.' Lindbergh promptly resigned his commission as a colonel in the U.S. Army Air Corps, writing that he saw 'no honorable alternative' given that Roosevelt had publicly questioned his loyalty."

After the Japanese attack on Pearl Harbor, Lindbergh sought to be recommissioned in the USAAF. The Secretary of War, Henry L. Stimson, declined the request on instructions from the White House. [Roosevelt could really hold a grudge.]

Unable to take on an active military role, Lindbergh approached a number of aviation companies and offered his services as a consultant. As a technical adviser with Ford in 1942, he was heavily involved in troubleshooting early problems encountered at the Willow Run

CHAPTER 15 CRUSADER FOR PEACE

Consolidated B-24 Liberator bomber production line. As B-24 production smoothed out, he joined United Aircraft in 1943 as an engineering consultant, devoting most of his time to its Chance-Vought Division. The following year, Lindbergh persuaded United Aircraft to designate him as a technical representative in the Pacific Theater to study aircraft performances under combat conditions. Among other things, he showed Marine pilots how to take off safely with a bomb load double the Vought F4U Corsair fighter-bomber's rated capacity. At the time, several Marine squadrons were flying bomber escorts to destroy the Japanese stronghold of Rabaul, New Britain, in the Australian Territory of New Guinea.

On May 21, 1944, Lindbergh flew his first combat mission: a strafing run near the Japanese garrison of Rabaul. In his six months in the Pacific in 1944, Lindbergh took part in fighter bomber raids on Japanese positions, flying 50 combat missions (again as a civilian). His innovations in the use of Lockheed P-38 Lightning fighters impressed a supportive Gen. Douglas MacArthur. Lindbergh introduced engine-leaning techniques to P-38 pilots, greatly improving fuel consumption at cruise speeds, enabling the long-range fighter aircraft to fly longer range missions. The famed flier visited the 475th in the summer of 1944, primarily to train the pilots in a technique for conserving fuel on long-distance missions. At that time, he met American Ace and future Medal of Honor recipient Thomas B. McGuire Jr.

"McGuire and Lindbergh spent time together, flying, fishing, and visiting local caves. McGuire even got so comfortable in their friendship, that one time he asked Lindbergh to get him a cup of coffee, much to the amusement of his more awestruck squadron mates. Apparently, the great man quietly fetched the brash young flier a hot cup of joe." (Sherman, 2011)

**Charles Lindbergh in the Pacific Theater 1944
Shown with American Ace and CMH Thomas B. McGuire Jr.**

FAIR USE: Its inclusion in the article adds significantly to the article because the photo and its historical significance are the object of discussion in the article.

The U.S. Marine and Army Air Force pilots who served with Lindbergh praised his courage and defended his patriotism. Charles Lindbergh passed away on August 26, 1974, in Kipahulu on the island of Maui, Hawaii."

Charles Lindbergh postponed the publishing of *The Wartime Journals of Charles Lindbergh* until a quarter century after the war, the better to attain "the objectivity that comes with years and the eyes of a new generation." His 1969 Introduction to the book provides a worthy retrospective: "We won the war in a military sense; But in a broader sense it seems to me we lost it, for our Western civilization is less respected and secure than it was

CHAPTER 15 CRUSADER FOR PEACE

before. In order to defeat Germany and Japan, we supported the still greater menaces of Russia and China --which now confront us in a nuclear weapon era. Poland was not saved. Much of our Western culture was destroyed. Meanwhile the Soviets have dropped their iron curtain to screen of Eastern Europe, and an antagonistic Chinese government threatens us in Asia. More than a generation after the war's end, our occupying armies must still occupy, and the world has not been made safe for democracy and freedom."

CHAPTER 16

LOUISE ARMSTRONG PASSING

The passing of his wife Louise would be a traumatic event for the Armstrong kids and their father. Charles, the youngest was kept pretty much in the dark. As he recalled many years later, "While I was an adolescent, several older relatives and family friends shared with me their observation that my relationship with my mother had been in one way noticeable. While other pre-or early-school kids might have been more diverted by an expanding world, I was content simply to sit and be with her for hours on end while she did her ironing and sewing. As a first grader, I didn't make much of my teacher's periodic comment 'How is your mother?' I took it as a greeting or friendly conversation rather than an inquiry. If I had recognized it as a question, I still wouldn't have known what to say. I answered, 'fine.' But I noticed that other adults were visiting mother with increasing frequency and paying her more than the usual attention. And I had noticed that she seemed physically uncomfortable much of the time. But I didn't ponder these facts, or draw conclusions, or even try. At six years, my experience had been that if adults were doing something, that something was the normal course of things. If they said it, it should be done or was true. My bouts with measles and chicken pox had taught me sickness was something that passed quickly. I took the behavior of a prolonged illness as just another experience.

But by the time of my September entry into the second grade, Mother had seemed uncomfortable far too long, even to my beginner's mind. The situation was troublesome to me. If her condition was normal,

CHAPTER 16   LOUISE ARMSTRONG PASSING

it was certainly an unpleasant sort of normal. But my observation that 'something is wrong' was still just 'something', not a formed idea about serious illness. I knew next to nothing about such things and certainly nothing of sickness not followed by wellness. Mother leaned on a chair when she walked about friends or couples. One woman or another seemed always to be with her, even while we were at home. Nobody had tried to explain to me or to eight-year-old Stanley that our mother had breast cancer, that she had already had surgery, and that she might get well but might not. I say 'tried to explain' since they may have anticipated my response to be, 'Cancer?'--What's that?' One might wonder, why not an age-appropriate clarification? My parents saw no reason to explain things in any thorough way to the boys who were off to college, so it's not surprising they kept the six and seven-year-olds in the dark. My parents were probably as open about personal matters as befit the time. But I think the reasons that they were not at all forthcoming was because they were in the dark. My brother Kay attended college and boarded at home, so it was obvious to him that mother was ill. But he was at a loss about its seriousness, at least for the first year. By the time I entered second grade, Kay suspected the truth. That's clear, for he offered my first intimation of mother's condition.

At bedtime one night, he told me she might not be with us much longer, so I must be sure to kiss her and tell her I love her. Whatever his wording, that was its drift. And whether fresh to the world or in denial, I had only the weakest grasp of the significance of what he said. It's not surprising that some of our most vivid memories are of first-time, 'what's-going-on-here?' experiences. I include in this species my first audience with a magician or a ventriloquist, first visit to a funeral home, first seeing an immersion baptism, first meeting a retarded person, and seeing *The Wizard of Oz* before I knew there was such a thing as fiction.

In each of these instances I knew something was mysterious indeed, and its strangeness paralyzed any capability I had to express my curiosity. So, it was with my mother's illness.

That year Harold Dryden, son of my mother's sister Lois, was the second of our first cousins to come live with us. This time it was only for his senior year since by then the southern Georgia school system provided up to grade eleven. Harold seemed eight feet tall to me, though he was a foot and two-thirds short of that. I watched Harold, summoned from football practice, help turn mother in bed, but I still didn't allow such particulars into my seven-year-old head as a threat to my world."

A few weeks after Charles started back to school, Harold's mother, Lois McCool Dryden, left her Waycross, Georgia, home to be with the family. O. K. was away on work assignments about as usual during his wife's illness. Later on, Charles would connect the pieces of his father's unusual behavior enough to settle on one word, "denial". "My beloved wife might die of breast cancer?" O. K. supposed her previous year's mastectomy was the end of the matter. It is highly improbable that there were false assurances by her surgeon and long-time friend Dr. Durward Hall. There were so many influences weighing on O. K.'s mind that one can only speculate as to which was heaviest. His family's doctrine had emphasized keeping or regaining health by right and proper living--health as a life path. A creed that had always served O. K. well, and from his vantage there was no reason to imagine that the outcome for his wife would be any less providential. The image of his sweetheart preparing to shuck her mortal coil was simply not coming and for many reasons.

79

CHAPTER 16   LOUISE ARMSTRONG PASSING

There was the comparative medical ignorance of the time. It is more likely his attitude was, "Now is not her time to leave."

To Charles his father's behavior would remain a mystery. ". . . I don't know how much was "conspiracy of emotion without reason" and how much was calling upon his religious faith. He was not given to simplifications regarding intervention by the Lord, but when it came to his adored wife he may have considerably qualified his world-view on ultimate and final matters."

Whatever his mental processes, it is clear that they distilled into a refusal-to-believe on the part of someone as much in love as on his wedding day. Much of the time he was away on research trips as customary. He had no savings and could do his assignment without first going to the source by traveling to Europe. On a normal day, nothing suited him better than to lead a quest to or from the headwaters of a journalistic stream, thereby gratifying with one effort two passions, crusading and writing. In his writings about his father, Charles would conclude, " . . . he was a man whose vision was distorted enough to justify going off to right the wrongs of a foreign continent while his life's only emotional intimate was in peril. The truth was invading the borders of his vital realm, so he strafed it from the fort he had emplaced around his consciousness."

In September O. K. departed for Europe to research material for a *Reader's Digest* series that would stoutly protest some of the U.S. government's post-war policies in Europe. He was expected to report to a Senate committee upon return. One of those policies was the destruction of Germany's industrial capability. O. K.'s attitude was: "The Nazis are gone. Revenge against the German people, who never were our enemy, helps no one and burdens our already heavy commitment to help reconstruct a despoiled Europe."

Another policy O. K. deemed entirely insane was the destruction of prime-of-life American aircraft following a four-power Allied agreement designed to please Berlin-based Soviet officials who had "insisted" on it. At an Allied airbase in Bavaria 2,000 fighters and bombers had been destroyed, and at another base the same fate for hundreds of P-47s. Some of these planes had seen only a few dozen flights or had only been flown a few hours. O. K. questioned the bureaucrats at the Office of Military Government in Berlin about the matter and got only a few evasions and (what the diplomats call) "untruths." A civilian-surplus worker questioned O. K.'s credentials for the probe. O. K. responded with a withering refresher course on the rights of citizens and taxpayers to know the fate of their property. O. K. then befriended a corporal, who drove him to an airbase outside Meierhausen. They arrived in time to witness the blowing up of a mile-long, wing-to-wing line of B-17s. In a newspaper article O. K. wrote: "The sight of these blasted airplanes is not stimulating to American pride or to our sense of security. Would any Congressman like to inspect about half a billion dollars (a lot of money in 1947) worth of sabotaged American glory? I can tell him where to look."

Boyd and Julia Dicus, among O. K. and Louise's best friends, became alarmed over Louise's declining condition. They found O. K. Junior as much in denial as Senior. Mr. Dicus wrote and showed Kay a preliminary cablegram to O. K. that read something like: "Louise failing; come home." Kay said, "But he would be horrified." Dicus replied "He needs to be horrified." The cable reached O. K. in Italy. He took the next

CHAPTER 16   LOUISE ARMSTRONG PASSING

train to Paris for the first flight home, only to face a strike by the Overseas Airline Pilots Association. He went on to London and with some calls to Washington got priority for the next transatlantic flight. He arrived at her bedside and clasped her hand. His loving voice roused Louise from a coma, and she mumbled her love to him. In minutes, she was gone.

Louise McCool Armstrong

Charles recalled, "The next day there was much bustle, with more than the ordinary number of visitors and relatives at work at home, all moving quickly about. An ambulance came and left. Mother was not home. I asked my sister Louise where mother was, and at fourteen years of age she can be excused for saying "downtown," but it left me all the more confused. The next day Dad took my brother, Stan and me 'downtown.' After he parked the car, we walked along a broad avenue where business and residential districts merged. We paused in front of what looked like a manor. We sat on the waist-high wall while Dad talked to us. 'Mother has gone to heaven.'"

By the time of their mother's death, the two oldest brothers had been discharged from the Navy and had entered college. Their sister Louise was fourteen and mature, but not enough to assume the keep of two little brothers and her school attendance. O. K. would have had to call in help even if he had not been away on business about half the time. His mother volunteered immediately. She had been widowed some months earlier, and her coming into the family home was symbiotic. Within months she fell, fracturing a hip.

Now there were three to care for. Total hip replacements were an image inside some orthopedist's head. But fortune's wheel would now turn so that the point fell on favor. O. K. found Mrs. Holsinger, a widow who would probably have given her age as "three score and ten." As Charles describes her, "Her language was as much Elizabethan as it was pure down-home Arkansas. Mrs. Holsinger's faith was Assembly-of-God. She read the Bible daily. She was warm, patient and in control. She understood children, partly because she was the matriarch of a populous clan. She had every quality one could want in a foster mother. Her only negative habit was to repeat the punch line of every story at least twice beyond the first telling (a habit perhaps more cultural than quirk). While interviewing Mrs. Holsinger, O. K. took board and room so much for granted, beyond her modest fee, that he didn't bring up the subject. He simply said, 'Now, let me show you to your room.' Her board and room

CHAPTER 16 — LOUISE ARMSTRONG PASSING

were more our benefit anyway, as she was quickly a member of the family by Act-of-Sentiment. Without her, those interim years could not have been as pleasant."

The family would carry on with heavy hearts. Even before his wife's passing, O. K. would guide his children using Bible passages before dinner. This would continue. It was a routine that was comforting to the family, but the kids would look forward to less formal instruction just before bedtime.

O. K.'s strength and warmth went far to make up for his frequent research and crusade absences. Until the children were well into the grades, he would tell them funny, attention-holding bedtime tales. He improvised these stories as he went along, sometimes recycling those told to the older children but restructuring just enough to entertain himself, often with satire on the current political scene.

Charles would later describe the personalities of some of the starring animals as "consistent with caricature: clever, conniving Fox; conniving Buzzard and sassy Wolf, comrades in lying and thievery; the disoriented Professor Owl, who tended to forget whose side he was on; Skunk, who protested wrongdoing in a manner only his kind could, hard-working Gopher; and confused but plodding Harry S. Donkey, that is until he took the alias of Jackass, the scheming politician. Some were original: Unlike Bugs Bunny, O. K.'s Rabbit was humble and shy and had to be brought out by the fostering leadership of the gang's patriarch, Ole Man Bear; and the stalwart, resourceful, clean-living Dudley Do-Right Hero, Florida Gator, who would subject himself to risky missions and save the day with the help of his loyal, trustworthy Lieutenant Hound. The plot and inevitable moral of each story were O. K.'s own, as were the ever-changing names, usually of politicians, he assigned to Fox, Wolf, and Buzzard depending on up-to-the-minute news of the world. We were too young to understand why he would go 'Ho, ho, ho' after giving 3 news-maker's names to that night's buzzard. He always kept the stories light, the worst transgressions by Fox, Buzzard and Wolf being their bungled attempts to deceive and trick their fellows of the kingdom.

There was no villainy mean enough to keep us awake. Justice prevailed at story's end (unless it was a serial installment), and the right-living animals would celebrate by sharing some of 'Ole Skunk's Firewater.' After the story, we would sing songs such as, 'My Old Kentucky Home', 'Way Down Upon the Suwannee River', 'When It's Springtime in the Rockies' or 'We Are the Boys of Old Florida, Down Where the Ole Gators Play'. It included 'Where the boys are the squarest and the girls are the fairest of any old state down our way…' In those days

CHAPTER 16 LOUISE ARMSTRONG PASSING

'square' didn't mean nerdish or prudish, it meant honest and truthful. After a song or two, the Lord's Prayer and lights out."

CHAPTER 17

THE CHANGING OF THE GUARD

Somewhat less than two years after his wife's death, O. K. brought home a guest, Marjorie E. Moore, editor of the Southern Baptist Convention's religious journal, *The Commission*. O. K. had known Marjorie since 1939. Soon after returning from Antarctica that year, Admiral Byrd asked O. K. to direct his public relations. O. K. already knew of Marjorie by professional reputation, so when he wrote an article titled "Peace Statesman" about the Admiral's adventures he called upon her to do the editing. In Marjorie's words, "Our friendship grew like the Constitution: article by article." Charles liked Marjorie.

Marjorie (Moore) Armstrong

In fact, when her weekend visit was coming to a close, he asked her in Dad's presence if she might arrange to return within, say, a month. "Splendid idea", responded O. K.. Mrs. Holsinger was entirely gracious to Marjorie (and Marjorie to her) and seemed accepting of this development. Her feelings weighed heavily with Charles. On any matter of consequence, including that of their Dad's courting a woman who might join the family, he regarded Mrs. Holsinger's opinion to be as legitimate as anyone else's excepting his dad's.

According to Charles, "After an interval of nearly two years Dad was bringing home a pleasant visitor. The marital potential of this new

CHAPTER 17 THE CHANGING OF THE GUARD

circumstance may have occurred to me, but that issue played second-string to the simple, good feeling that Dad now had a nice companion, and all of us had someone who seemed to make the scene more complete. Maybe I had a new companion too, but I certainly didn't try to put Marjorie on the balance opposite mother. I didn't think, 'Here's a new mother,' nor did I think, 'Nice, but not a new mother.' I didn't deliberate the matter. It felt appropriate; it felt good. It didn't take analysis to feel a void in the family. Stan's void, the same as mine, was partially but comfortably filled by our adored Mrs. Holsinger. Dad's was filled only by work until Marjorie came along. I entered the fourth grade that fall, and soon thereafter the plans for their wedding began."

After Louise died, O. K. didn't try to find another "true love", probably for at least two reasons. He may have written it off as too unlikely, too far-fetched. It is more likely that he didn't want anyone to replace his "first and only and always love". The intimate place in his life had been taken; the body left, but the spirit stayed. One small illustration of this was his ritual with letters to family. (Letter writing was the way of the day: To most, but especially to a Scottish journalist during the Great Depression, telephoning was an expensive indulgence compared with typed correspondence.) As the fifth child, Charles would receive the fourth carbon, so there was no reading it in dim light.[4] Until his last years, O. K. enclosed in these "Dear Children" letters a little sprig of Lilies-of-the-Valley, Louise's favorite flower, which he would pick from our back yard. At any pretext, slight or grand (such as a meaningful date on the

---

[4] See Letter to Kay Armstrong in References

calendar), he would make a loving reference to her in the letter. Marjorie must have had occasion to notice these unrelenting reminders.

With his real mate gone, his intention was to find someone to meet practical needs. His emotions would adjust to realities. He wanted someone highly efficient and competent. O. K. was continually traveling the country and the world on political crusades and *Readers Digest* research missions. His life lacked organization. He would forget his hat, make it to the airport just in time, misplace a bill, and never shop for clothes. In Marjorie, he saw system and order to the needed measure and beyond. And, he knew, with her comparative youth (late thirties, nineteen years his junior), she would keep things organized. And organize she did. Within weeks of Marjorie's joining the family the talents sought by O. K. were on display, including some reforms he did not foresee, and at least one he almost didn't notice: Marjorie bought O. K. clothes for him on the sly. He wouldn't spend for himself--on clothing or much of anything else. He also wanted nothing he wore to draw attention by quality (too cheap or too fine), color or style. There was accordingly a sameness to his outfits. This allowed Marjorie to buy clothes for him, clip the tags, and slip them into the closet where he would reach for them without a thought and none the wiser.

Mrs. Holsinger was impressed by such clandestine goings-on. She had always been entirely adaptable to O. K.'s almost literally fly-by-night schedule--off on a political crusade here, a research trip there. Marjorie wouldn't try to change that, but she would arrange pertaining circumstances and the home milieu to fit.

Marjorie's diligent efforts to keep O. K. to his schedule, home and away, were generally successful. While she couldn't rescind Murphy's

CHAPTER 17   THE CHANGING OF THE GUARD

Law, she made sure departure preliminaries didn't overlap departure time. No more arriving at the airport while the DC-3's props are already whirring.

Marjorie bought him a bigger desk and a proper typewriter. She learned and remembered names. At a convention, for example, O. K. and Marjorie would come across an acquaintance. Marjorie: "O. K., you remember Robert and Jane Remington . . ." O. K.: "Yes, of course ..." Her skills at editing were such that the experts at the *Reader's Digest* left O. K.'s manuscripts at her word and bothered only with Digest-style condensation. Most of her organizing efforts came off much more predictably when O. K. was out of town, his presence being something of a disruption of the rhythm. An example was afternoon tea, which she dreamed up as a home-from-grade-school greeting for Stanley and Charles. O. K. wasn't opposed to it, but when he was home it often didn't fit. By the time Stan and Charles reached later grades, there were other things to do after school. According to Charles, "The after-school tea parties never fit."

[My wife, Pamela (Wilcox) Capages remembers the Armstrong family when they attended University Heights Baptist Church in Springfield, Missouri in the late 1960s and later. According to Pamela, "My earliest recollection of Mr. Armstrong was listening to a presentation he made at my church on missionary work. I do not recall the details. I do remember his two sons, Charles and Stanley who sang in the choir along with my sister, Sandy. My sister had a crush on one of the brothers, both were very good-looking boys. But I remember Marjorie quite well. Marjorie sang in the adult choir. She invited me to join the Women's Missionary Union or WMU. She was serving as the President of the WMU at the time and asked me to make a presentation to the group. She knew that I had drawn a pencil sketch of Jesus that was inspired by the famous 1940 portrait by Warner Sallman. That beautiful painting of Jesus was hanging on one of the interior walls of the church. (It is my understanding that it still hangs on that wall to this day.) The sketch that I made was used with the children's Sunday school class.

One time after church, Marjorie came up to me for a chat. As she was singing in the church choir, she had noticed that I was chewing gum during the service. She said, 'You know, that is not very becoming of you to chew gum during the service.' Oh my, I was taken by surprise and a wee bit embarrassed at her directness, but I knew even then that she had aspired to see something greater in me. Marjorie's comment left an indelible impression on me. Today, before slipping a piece gum in my mouth, which I rarely do now, I again think of Marjorie-- my inspirational WMU leader."

Later on, Pamela would once again draw a pencil sketch of Jesus and it would be included in a book of her poetry called WILDWOOD PSALMS. When my wife mentioned the chewing gum incident to Kay Armstrong in 2018, he quipped, "Well, that was Marjorie for sure."]

CHAPTER 18

BACK TO POLITICS

When O. K. decided to run for the U. S. Congress, he had already served several terms in the Missouri Legislature. Many of his Missouri state legislative colleagues had routinely come to him for help with the wording of legislation. In 1938 Governor Stark had called upon him to serve as one of two secret agents with the assignment of investigating and undermining the Pendergast machine of Kansas City. The Governor was familiar with O. K.'s work as a legislator and with his syndicated 1934 exposé titled "Feed 'Em and Vote 'Em," which uncovered Boss Tom Pendergast's vice network in Kansas City.

In a cover letter to the publishers, O. K. wrote: "My greatest difficulty was keeping the length down. A book could be written about this most powerful city boss in America (Pendergast was a political boss, not so much into the violence of the Capone type underworld mobs). There is no doubt about this coming election doing just what I say in the story --it will clinch his control of the state to an absolute degree. His control is quite different from that of Huey Long, as you know. We hit it squarely with the Long story, and I hope, hereby, to keep up my reputation for prophetic revelation."

Pendergast's political machine owned a huge cement enterprise. The Kansas City sidewalks became six feet deep! He picked and trained police officers who would arrest motorists at random and run them through the courts to shake them down for imaginary transgressions, and he appointed judges who would kowtow to these proceedings. Another

CHAPTER 18　　BACK TO POLITICS

shakedown was to force city employees to "donate" two days' pay per week to the machine. Purchasing agents would rotate the take. One competing vendor of food for the jail would play the game by bidding absurdly high and 'lose' it that month. Another vendor, whose turn it was to be "it", would be low bidder that round, but his bid would be high enough to allow a kickback to the political machine. Bidding would be restricted to those firms who agreed to play the game, each in its turn every fourth month.

Dewitt Wallace of the *Digest* reminded O. K. that a politician or two in very high places on the other side of the fence owed his job to Boss Pendergast and to brace himself for an I.R.S. hit at some point.

[In a speech to the U.S. House of Representatives in May 1952, O. K. said: "It was apparent to me that unless an aroused public worked against this machine it would continue to rule and to spread its corruption."]

In January 1939, he testified on his findings to a Jackson County grand jury, Judge Allen Southern presiding. In 1947, O. K. wrote for the *Readers Digest* "Kansas City's Boss-Busting Editor," about the newspaperman with the courage to reveal the gangster activities in print.

Governor Stark warned O. K. that, in revenge for his crusade, the Kansas City branch of the I.R.S. now or later would go after him. Especially if he ran for Congress.

The most time-consuming phase of the campaign was driving through the rural seventh district of southwest Missouri in a "sound-truck," an old car with megaphone-shaped speakers mounted on top. While the Marine band played from 78 rpm records, they would pull up to the town square, a crowd would gather and candidate Armstrong would give his stump speech. In her graduate thesis on O. K., Ms.

Sirianni wrote: "He was an encyclopedia of knowledge in many different fields. His oratory could stir the blood of ordinary farm folks, or he could speak in front of the most educated people." And at a convention or banquet he could hold forth after no more than this notice: "O. K., do you mind offering a few words; say, twenty, thirty minutes' worth?" O. K.: "I'd be delighted. When do I go on?" (The time is 7:40) "How about 7:45'?". O. K.: "Excellent."

He always invited follow-up questions, and on the campaign trail these pertained to such issues as the Marshall Plan, the Soviet Union, inflation, debt, farmers issues and so on. A group of college students supporting O. K. heard that Will Rogers Jr. was coming to Springfield to make a speech in behalf of O. K.'s opponent, the incumbent. They contacted Mr. Rogers and urged him to debate Mr. Armstrong, and to do that with the media present. Of course he would. But when the incumbent's managers heard about this, they contacted Rogers and reminded him that he had never heard Armstrong at the lectern, and they told him they were cancelling the debate. Meanwhile the incumbent Congressman made the mistake of

On the Campaign Trail
Kay, Charles, Stanley, O.K., and Marjorie

CHAPTER 18   BACK TO POLITICS

agreeing to a series of debates with O.K., but, after the first debate in which the incumbent was humiliated, he failed to show for the second debate and cancelled the remaining. O. K. won the election.

After the election, there was an interim while O. K. and Marjorie searched for a home in the Washington area. By January they found a small house in West Haven near Bethesda, MD.

Members of the U.S. House of Representatives were allowed staffs of three: two secretaries and an administrative assistant. The Congressional office-supply store had a "robotyper." This innovation was quite a leap. With the robotyper, one could punch a bunch of selectable paragraphs into a magazine.

There were as many magazines as points to make or topics. The first magazine of the semi-form letter would have a "Dear Constituent" opening and introductory paragraph. A separate magazine provided the closing paragraph on each issue. The center paragraphs could be magazine or individualized. After punching in those magazines, the robotyper would type out your letter except for the tailor-made portion.

The pressure of being a Congressman in Washington D. C. was overwhelming and O. K. would suffer from periods of depression and would self-impose his own hospitalization at one point. The brothers, Kay and Stanley have different recollections than Charles for this time in their father's life. But a lapse into depression is certainly understandable when viewed in the light of today's political environment and the lack of Government common sense. Perhaps things haven't changed very much after all. We just have pharmaceuticals for treatment in lieu of hospitalization. Once more, O. K. would be ahead of his time. As Stanley recalls, "Dad realized he was not insane, but simply depressed."

CHAPTER 19

THE KOREAN WAR

By the time the 82nd Congress opened in January 1951, Congressman O. K. Armstrong had become thoroughly disgusted with the direction of the Korean war since the entry of the Communist Chinese. The Chinese had invaded South Korea, and instead of meeting them with a mailed fist, the Truman administration was extending them a limp wrist. The conflict was being waged with a "stalemate or defeat" strategy, featuring unprecedented engagement restrictions ranging from the bizarre to the absurd. These restrictions resulted in maximizing allied casualties and precluded success. In their effort to fathom this baffling policy, some believed that certain U.S. State Department leaders were beholden to special European economic interests who did not want to offend Communist China and, thereby, compromise trade. Others speculated that the administration simply didn't want to offend Communist China, period. Whatever the reason, it was clear to O. K. that the war was being run by civilian fools.

O. K. provides a fair scan of his world view in this section of his book, *The Fifteen Decisive Battles of the United States* which portrays American history from General Oglethorpe's defense of his Georgia colony at Bloody Marsh in 1742 to the Battle of Midway. The Foreword is dated 1961:

"I resumed this study after World War II had ushered in the new and terrifying era --the atomic age, which quickly mushroomed into the thermonuclear age. It is still my purpose to honor those who bore the

CHAPTER 19   THE KOREAN WAR

battle, whether their cause triumphed or not; to show how the brave met the brave; and how the skill of commanders, the steadfastness of officers, the courageous obedience of armed men on land or sea, led to victory or, by the turn of fortune, met defeat. But another and more compelling purpose prompts me to present the accounts of the decisive battles of American arms: It affords the opportunity to point out the stark fact that war is now completely obsolete. As a method of resolving differences between governments of sovereign nations, which today means between entire populations, war is the ultimate in futility and absurdity.

The author shares the profound conviction of people of good will everywhere that the supreme task of humanity is to prevent war in the present and the future. The great challenge of this age for those who believe in the preservation of a way of life in which people may enjoy liberty and the pursuit of happiness is to make war impossible. It can be done -and it must be done. It will mean abandoning fear and appeasement of the evil force that, through the mistakes of the victorious powers in World War II, allowed the worldwide domination of the countries of eastern Europe and allowed the Communist menace to spread from the Soviet Union to mainland China, Manchuria, the northern parts of Korea, Vietnam and Tibet; and to eventually threaten millions more peoples with its aggressive designs in every area of the globe.

The task will mean meeting the present challenge of a regime based on atheistic materialism, dedicated to stamping out all freedom of the individual citizen and his collective liberties, with our determined announcement that this world cannot endure half-slave and half-free, and that those of the free world will never cease their efforts for human liberty until all the world is free. It will call for the steadfast endeavors of those who, with courage and initiative, will fashion the new tools needed to build a lasting peace.

The peace that humanity seeks must replace the international anarchy of the mid-twentieth century with order under law. It must improve upon the United Nations, reshaping that organization into an instrument whereby its high aims and objectives can be realized instead of thwarted by the enemies of peace, a forum where simple truth can prevail over vicious propaganda, a parliament whose constructive action cannot be vetoed by aggressors who thrive upon conflict and disorder.

The structure of peace that we must build, if we are not all to perish together, must be based upon these four great foundation stones of liberty, equal justice under national and international law, collective security to prevent the rise of lawless aggressors, and a brotherhood of those who recognize and utilize for the common good those spiritual and moral values without which all else will fail.

If, in addition to building a protection for our own lives and for those of future generations, we desire to honor those in the past years who were willing to pay their 'last full measure of devotion' to the country asking this bounty of them, we will assume without delay our responsibilities in this great task."

Of O. K.'s precepts, a most pointed one was, "Peace is not founded upon disarmament; Peace is founded upon liberty and justice." A derivative principle was to rid the world of totalitarianism. South Carolina Congressman William Jennings Bryan Dorn shared O. K.'s view that the Korean War could be won with proper military appliance, including the use of Nationalist troops. O. K. recalled a meeting with the House

CHAPTER 19   THE KOREAN WAR

Foreign Affairs Committee during which Dorn needled Secretary of State Dean Acheson with, "Mr. Secretary, are we going to win that war?"

The following are comments by Major General John K. Singlaub[5] that Charles Armstrong transcribed from tape. General Singlaub would later command U.S. Forces in South Korea:

General Singlaub

According to General Singlaub, "As early as 1927, Chiang Kai-shek knew that Soviet adviser Borodin was there not to help China but to help Mao Tse-Tung and the Communists, and for that reason threw Borodin out. Chiang needed means to resist the revolution which had been started by Sun Yat-sen. Our State Department refused financial support, and on that account, Chiang had to make deals with the bankers of Shanghai.

The U.S. State Department was actively supporting Communist China and had been doing so since before the end of World War II. President Truman sent General Marshall on the Marshal Mission to China to bring the Communists and Nationalists together."

J. M. Roberts, CBE of Warden at Merton College, Oxford University related the following: "The 38th parallel (dividing North Korea from South Korea) was conjured up in 1945 as an administrative boundary to divide the responsibility of disarming Japanese forces, to be done by Soviet forces north of the line, by American troops south thereof. Plans for reunification were referred to the United Nations.

---

[5] See Singlaub in References

Efforts were made to hold elections for Korea as a unit. These failed, so the United Nations. recognized a government established in the south as the legitimate government of the Republic of Korea. But by then the Soviet zone had a government claiming general sovereignty. Russian and American troops withdrew in May 1949."

In January 1950 Dean Acheson, in a speech to the National Press Club in Washington, declared, "Taiwan Indo-China and Korea to be outside the American 'Containment' perimeter.' Acheson implied that he did not see a Communist China as worrisome since China and the Soviet Union would be rivals. After all, the Russians had taken the Chinese provinces of Mongolia and Manchuria. So, why antagonize China by protecting Taiwan, Indo-China and Korea? Acheson was unaware that negotiations were underway leading to the Soviets returning the Manchurian railway and Port Arthur to China. [Johnson] Stalin dealt with Mao's new government by taking advantage of Acheson's green light on Korea. Stalin reasoned that a war in Korea would teach Mao who his true friends were and establish Chinese military dependence on the Soviet Union. Stalin signaled North Korean Communist Dictator Kim Ill-sung to start a limited aggression across the 38th Parallel

But on June 25, 1950, Kim invaded the south, not with Stalin's probe, but with full force. President Truman, acting on behalf of the U.N., responded immediately. We were able to get the U.N. force committed because the Soviets had walked out in 1950 and were not there to veto. MacArthur's perspective was that all Korea was open to Allied military operations.

Another interview by O. K. was with Harry G. Summers Jr. Summers was an infantry colonel in the United States Army and had

CHAPTER 19   THE KOREAN WAR

served as a squad leader in the Korean War. In that interview recorded by O. K. and transcribed from tape by O. K.'s son (Charles), Colonel Summers recalls, " In July the U.S. and its allies fell back into defensive lines along the Naktong River, a strategy designed to buy time until proper forces could be mobilized. By September, the buildup was complete, allowing the allies to assume the strategic offensive with MacArthur's brilliantly planned Inchon invasion. The Eighth Army, breaking out from the Pusan perimeter, forced the North Korean Army into retreat. Within three months Allied forces under MacArthur had pushed well north of the 38th Parallel and had retaken Seoul. On October 19, 1950, North Korea's capital Pyongyang was captured. On Oct. 21 the 17th Infantry Regiment of the 7th Infantry Division, U.S. X Corps, reached the Yalu River on the Manchurian border in eastern Korea. In the west, the U.S. Eighth Army was also nearing the Manchurian border. [At the time, Col. Harry Summers was a sergeant in the 24th Infantry Division's 21st Infantry Regiment 18 miles from Sinuiju, on the Yalu River.] In his words, "North Korean forces were surrendering in droves."

When American-U.N. forces closed in on the Manchurian frontier on the Yalu, the Chinese intervened. [Singlaub] A half million Chinese troops had crossed the border and were in the mountains of North Korea. [Summers]: On Nov.1, the 130,000-man Chinese XIII Army Group struck the Eighth Army, destroying the 1st Cavalry Division's 8th Cavalry Regiment and forcing the entire army into retreat. [Singlaub]: With a major offensive in November and December, they overran our Second Infantry Division on the northern west coast close to the Yalu. [Summers]: On Nov. 25, in the east, China's 120,000-man IX Army Group attacked X Corps, destroying the 7th Infantry Division's 31st

Infantry Regiment and [in December] forcing the 1st Marine Division into its famous fighting retreat from the Chosin Reservoir. [Singlaub]: They hit the 10th Corps located in Hung-Nau north of the big port of Huan-San. That Chinese offensive forced the 10th Corps to withdraw all their troops from North Korea back to South Korea. The 8th Army, located up near the border, did an orderly withdrawal of its forces from the west coast. [Summers]: By January. 1, 1951, the U.S. and its allies had been forced out of North Korea. On January 4, 1951, the South Korean capital of Seoul once again fell to the enemy.

[Singlaub]: General Walker was killed during this offensive against Seoul. General Matthew Ridgway was sent in to replace him. Ridgway developed a plan to stabilize the attack and to blunt it south of the Hann River south of Seoul, which he did in major battles.

Then when the Chinese reached south of Seoul, General Ridgway started his U.N. counter-offensive. Ridgway worked wonders with the Eighth Army. By the end of January 1951, the U.N. forces were on the move again. Seoul was recaptured in March. Ridgway drove the Chinese back close to what is now the Demilitarized Zone. Soviet U.N. representative Malik offered to negotiate.

[Summers] Allied forces were ordered to fall back into a tactical defensive and a strategic defensive as well, giving up any plans to drive north again. The best one can hope for in a strategic defensive is a stalemate --victory was ruled out. This prospect induced General MacArthur to write House Minority Leader Joseph Martin a letter with the famous "In war there is no substitute for victory."

Major General John K. Singlaub states: "When we entered the Korean war, the administration assigned to our command senior Army

CHAPTER 19   THE KOREAN WAR

officers who had spent their careers in quartermaster or staff assignments and had never seen combat. The Chinese Communists "ran circles around them." Everything we did seemed as if ordered by the Communists. The Communists had quickly made the 38th Parallel into a boundary, which colored all thinking in the U.S. State Department. Anything suggestive of adjusting that line to make it more defensible was vetoed. The Truman administration established numerous other disabling restrictions: The Truman administration denied the U.S. Navy the authority to interdict vessels going from China to the port of (sounds like) Ab-doo. I was deputy commander of the Joint Advisory Commission of Korea, the CIA's covert action unit, and I had a maritime unit. We made it very unpleasant for the Chinese to try to make that crossing. We captured a lot of their cargo ships and hurt the North Korean economy. That had to be done as covert action. But the Navy could have easily closed off those ports in North China. By that time, we knew the Chinese were in. Chinese propaganda would have it that these troops were volunteers, but they were not. The excuse for some of our restrictions was that the Chinese delegates to the United Nations claimed that their troops had no connection with the Chinese government.

There was a restriction prohibiting any amphibious end run. We had done that in the initial attack. After Inchon, we pulled out a couple of divisions, including Marine divisions from Inchon, and moved them to the East Sea (the Sea of Japan) and landed a force of marines and the 3rd Infantry Division from Japan, landing at Huan-San. We had the 7th and 3rd Infantry Division and a Marine Division. Two Korean divisions were under the 10th corps and pushed up to the border, surrounding and neutralizing large numbers of North Koreans. That was the situation when the Chinese intervention occurred in November 1950. The restrictions against going north were placed on the commander so that after we withdrew all the forces from North Korea in late Decenber1950, we were not permitted to contemplate an encircling movement. We had the amphibious advantage; Amphibious landings on the west coast are very difficult because of the World's second largest tidal action, at 31 feet, second only to Canada's Bay of Fundi with 32 feet. This exposes miles of mud flats over which vehicles have no mobility. The Inchon landing was an engineering miracle; the force had to land at high tide, and then wait until the next high tide for reinforcements.

MacArthur's Inchon invasion was a major victory for the U. S., but forces were prohibited from attacking the Chinese airfields north of the Yalu River, mostly in Manchuria. An-Dung was a port city at the mouth of the Yalu. Immediately to the north and west of An-Dung were three of their principal airfields. There were many others, but the most important were there close to the border at the river. We were prohibited from taking out those airfields, thus providing sanctuary for the forces killing our troops, when they certainly offered us none. These airfields were in China, but the aircraft were flown by Russians. Stalin had sent an entire aviation corps, consisting of an air-defense division and two Mig-15 air divisions made up of Russia's best pilots. Most of these pilots became Stalin's heroes by fighting Hitler's remnants after the Luftwaffe had been reduced to old men and teenagers with experience far too meager to put up a decent dogfight. In Korea, our Saber Jet pilots shot down nine of these Russian Migs for each U. S. aircraft lost. The North Koreans and Chinese had access to China; I f they were pushed anywhere near the border, all they had to do was step over the border and make faces at our troops.

CHAPTER 19   THE KOREAN WAR

MacArthur was never allowed to make division-sized attacks. [Singlaub] Meanwhile, Taiwan's forces were eager to join the effort. They recognized that the Communists were a threat to all Asia, not just Korea. We refused to allow Chinese Nationalists to pursue them. MacArthur objected to this and to these restrictions against going north and to sanctuary in China. President Truman had made a clear-cut decision about that, and MacArthur went around the President to Congress in hopes they would change the restriction policy. MacArthur spoke openly about the matter.

In April 1951, Congressmen O. K. and Dorn flew to Korea to design a plan to win the war and keep Korea free and unified. O. K. intended to return to Congress and "hold their feet to the fire."

In her thesis, Ms. Sirianni capably reports on the scene: "Congressmen Armstrong and Dorn forfeited their Easter recess and paid half the airfare to see the conflict in Korea for themselves and report to the American people. According to the 1951 Congressional Record, Armstrong and Dorn made a good team. Dorn was young, aggressive and gregarious. Armstrong was older and more reserved, a former university professor, an accomplished author, lecturer, and byline staff writer for the *Reader's Digest*.

Thirty years later, at the age of almost 88, O. K.'s memories were fresh. "Fellow Congressman Dorn and I were not at all satisfied with what was going on in Korea. This was April 1951. We had had a briefing on the war by Secretary of State Dean Acheson. The best he could do with it was to say that 'We're in this war with allies, and we have to cooperate with them, in particular the British.' Acheson's idea was not to win the Korean war but to hold the Communists to a stalemate at a battle line, World War I style.

Acheson was also loyal to British motives, which principally centered about trade. The British wanted to trade with Red China. They wanted to trade with anybody willing to trade with them, regardless of politics or principles. And I think the British then, as of now and forever, were for trade over all else. Also, I think that it was so fixed in Acheson's mind that we should not win a war --that would be bad for our image. But if we hold them, they'll get discouraged and stop." That disastrous theory was picked up by President Johnson and Robert MacNamara during the Vietnam war.

"In any case, I attended this briefing. At the close of the briefing, a young man introduced himself to me as William Jennings Bryan Dorn of South Carolina. He was as exasperated as I was. So, he and I decided to give up our Easter vacation in order to go to Korea, see the war in person, and draw up a plan if we could. I had already drawn up my own outline of the fundamentals, which I considered to be: the removal of sanctuaries; the destruction of the bridges along the Yalu; destruction of all enemy airfields; authorization for offensive action against Communist troops; and authorization to ignore artificial boundaries such as the 38th Parallel

Now bear in mind, we paid our own way. We flew to Japan and then to Korea. The Air Force showed us every courtesy. Dorn had served in the Army Air Corps. I had helped to start the Aviation Section in World War I that developed into the Army Air Corps and then into the Air Force. The man in charge of the Far East Wing of the Air Force was General Stratemeyer of Orlando. He assigned a plane to us, and we were flown all over South Korea, and we saw the fighting clear up to where they were dropping the napalm bombs."

CHAPTER 19   THE KOREAN WAR

Addressing the House of Representatives on May 3, 1951, O. K. recounted his visit: "For a little more than three weeks, Congressman Dorn and I were privileged to inspect most of our military installations in Japan, the bases, camps, the fighting front of the Korean war and the strength of the Nationalist Chinese forces on Formosa. Right on the battle line, we had the unique privilege of talking to the commander of the Eighth Army in Korea, General Matthew Ridgway. The war was real as we stood at the front-line north of Seoul and observed the engagement between our doughboys and enemy troops just across the river. We talked to scores of high-ranking officers of all branches of the service, including Generals McArthur, Stratemeyer and Ridgeway. We also talked to scores of American GIs. We gained an accurate cross-section of their opinions.

We are not here to debate how we got into the tragic war in Korea, although it is quite clear that there would have been no Korean War had it not been for the vast mistakes in our foreign policies since the victory of the free world in Europe and the Far East in the Second World War.

The people of our nation are asking anxiously, 'Are we doomed to perpetual war, with all its costs and losses? Can we never have peace as past generations knew it?' Certainly, if this Nation and the world are ever to have a just and lasting peace again it will be because of new, firm, workable policies based on justice and honor instead of expediency and appeasement. We should formulate and announce those policies now.

Three things struck us square in the face as we saw the grim fighting in Korea. First, the losses in this war are the greatest for the number of men engaged of any in American history. Second, our boys are fighting bravely in the hope they might speedily win the war, despite the handicaps forced upon them by our short-sighted policies. Third, in this undeclared war military strategy is subordinated to political expediency.

Many of our allies are dealing in war materials with the enemy. Members of the United Nations that have branded Red China an aggressor before all mankind are still carrying on a lucrative trade with those who kill our men on the battlefield. Strange as it may seem, our own soldiers, those who fight and die for freedom's cause, are not permitted to strike the enemy at his bases and centers of transport and communication beyond Korea. And most astonishing of all, our allies, the free Chinese, those who fought the Communists long before we did, are neutralized and not permitted to help win the war against the tyrants that oppress their own country. Although the Nationalist government is still the recognized member of the United Nations, and a permanent member of the Security Council, the military forces of that government must stand idle in Formosa for fear of offending some of the appeasers of the criminal regime. Bear in mind that the announced objective of the United Nations when we went into Korea was not to stop the fighting at the 38th parallel; it was to unite Korea as an independent nation.

"I submit that there are three things we can do in Korea and the Far East.

First, we can withdraw from the war, thus turning Korea and eventually all of Asia, including Japan, over to the Communists. This would mean the utter defeat of our first at collective security. Such an action would be branded as dishonorable in the eyes of history for all time to come.

Second, we can end the war by negotiating with the aggressors. We can sit and talk and wait and talk some more. We can dicker with 'these

CHAPTER 19   THE KOREAN WAR

underlings of the Kremlin.' This is what Stalin and his stooges would like for us to do. But the 'peace' they would promise would be false, and the price they would demand would be too high. This seems to be the course the British Socialist Government would have us take. On the very day I arrived in Formosa, the day on which General MacArthur was recalled, Mr. Shinwell announced in Parliament that his government would insist upon three conditions: That the Red Chinese be given a seat in the United Nations; that Formosa be turned over to the Communist Chinese; and that the Communist regime be permitted to help write the treaty of Peace with Japan. To seat the Red Chinese in the United Nations would be to denounce every ideal of its charter. To turn Formosa over to these enemies of freedom would mean that all the Nationalist Chinese, military and civilian, would be slaughtered. To allow these international outlaws to help write the treaty with Japan would be to throw away what is left of the victory in World War II. That such suggestions could come from any official of a once proud and powerful nation is unspeakably tragic.

When I conferred with Generalissimo Chiang Kai-shek, he asked me: 'Does the discharge of General MacArthur mean that your government is ready to adopt a policy of abandoning us?' I assured him that whatever the administration policy might be, there would be those of us in Congress and among the people of this country who can never forget the historic friendship between us and China and who will never turn our backs on those who fight for liberty and justice. Yes, we can end the war by shameful retreat, or by compromise and appeasement. Or, our third option, we can go ahead and win the victory free men deserve.

I tried conscientiously to find the answer as to whether we can win the war in Korea promptly and finally. I say to you that we can. We can win if we adopt a new program of firm, vigorous, intelligent action to establish a just and lasting peace in all the Far East and ultimately in all the world. In order to bring the fighting in Korea to an end, we must apply pressure on the following categories -- political, propaganda, and military. We must utilize political pressure that brands Soviet Russia an aggressor for sponsoring and supporting this war and that warns her enslaving regime that it must stop the war in Korea or be ostracized by the breaking- off of diplomatic and trade relations. Propaganda pressure should start with the announcement of the willingness of free people to work constantly for the liberation of those now enslaved by the communist world.

Militarily, we and our allies must do four things: First, we must enforce a blockade against the entire mainland of China. This should have been done long ago. It should have been done on the day the Red Chinese entered the war. Instead, most of our allies have continued trade with Red China as usual.

You were shocked, and the whole country was shocked, by the announcement a few days ago that since the beginning of the Communist aggression in Korea last June, 120,000 tons of rubber have passed from British Malaya into Red China, all of it to feed the Communist war machine and much of it passing right on into Soviet Russia. This was just one item in a long list of strategic war materials being supplied our enemies. Tin, steel products, machine tools, airplane engines, motor vehicles --numerous such commodities are imported regularly into Red China by ships flying flags of the free nations.

In Formosa, I was given the information by Chinese intelligence officers (and doubtless such information is in the hands of our government) indicating that some time ago the Soviet government began

CHAPTER 19   THE KOREAN WAR

construction of an atomic bomb plant in northwestern China, near the Soviet border, and that nearly all the material needed for that plant has been supplied by our allies who are supposed to be fighting aggression. This is a shameful betrayal. It will not be enough for an aroused public opinion to force a halt to the shipment of war materials. We should blockade the entire Chinese coast. We should cut off all communication and trade. We should make the embargo so tight that not even a fishing smack can get through. If we do that the armies of Communist General Mao would face starvation. This is our first step to make them lay down their arms and quit the fight.

Second, we should permit and encourage use of the Nationalist Chinese troops now idle on Formosa. On this recent trip, I visited and inspected thousands of these troops of all branches. They are marking time, eager to get back into the fight. How long are we going to send our boys to slaughter while able and willing Chinese soldiers are not permitted to fight for their own country's freedom?

General MacArthur advocated use of these troops. He did not advocate engaging our land armies on the mainland of China. He did not want the weakening of the defenses of Formosa. He pled for utilizing Generalissimo Chiang and his troops in any practical and effective way. For this he was denounced by our administration. Yet, MacArthur is right --this is a logical step in ending the Korean War in victory.

Third, we should encourage and support the guerrillas within Red China, to offer every possible resistance to their oppressors. According to intelligence given me in Taipei, there are more than a million of these loyal Chinese underground fighters for freedom ready to harass the Reds, to foment rebellion and to assist in the overthrow of the Soviet-dominated government. Let us encourage them in every way possible.

Let us promise them arms and ammunition. Let us assure them they will be supported.

Fourth, we should permit United Nations forces to bomb military targets in Manchuria and China. Note that I said military targets. I shall never advocate bombing of civilian peoples. For the common people everywhere are the victims of war. It was so in past wars, and it is so in this one. I watched the dropping of napalm bombs in Korea. The bombs are made of jellified gasoline, and upon exploding they literally burn up everything within range. It is utterly tragic that in this war of attrition we are having to destroy so many Korean people-- and their homes and workshops. What a way to "liberate" people. We can stop that by bombing the railroads and supply lines and military bases of Manchuria and along the China coast. The war is being fought from Manchuria, where the heavy arms industry is manned partly by Japanese prisoners of war that Russia refused to repatriate. From Manchuria, the war implements are brought into Korea.

Congressman Dorn and I heard from Allied soldiers of all ranks, including our Canadian friends. They know that if it were not for the build-up in Manchuria, if it were not for the plants where those MIG planes are built and for the tanks and for the guns manufactured there, they could not carry on the war in North Korea.

Soldiers cannot fight without food and ammunition. The Communists cannot fight in Korea and at the same time fight the guerrillas and stave off invasions at every point on their coast. They cannot fight without bases and supplies. With their transportation lines, bases, and airfields destroyed, it would be impossible for the Red Chinese to mass again and cross the Yalu River for another offensive.

CHAPTER 19   THE KOREAN WAR

Congressman Dorn and I met with General Ridgway near the battle line. As he stood with his battle map in his hands, I asked him the question, 'General, can we win this war under our present handicaps?' He answered, 'We can hold them, I feel sure, and we can drive them back. But we cannot win a military victory this way.' That statement was supported by every high-ranking officer and by every GI that we talked to. I could quote by name many other generals who expressed the same opinion as Ridgway. I could--but I shall not, for I do not want any more generals fired. Not one of them said we could win this war of attrition – by this operation 'meat grinder.'

Look what we have to gain by a positive program. Not only may we win victory in Korea; we can overthrow the Communist regime in China. And that would be the greatest victory over the world-wide conspiracy of Soviet communism since our misguided leaders began their policies of appeasement and collaboration in 1943. It would be the Kremlin's first significant setback since the dismal betrayals of the rights and interests of free men at the conferences of Tehran, Yalta and Potsdam. With all steps in this program taken, the war could be ended in a few months. I tell you, we and our allies can end this war–in victory.

Such can be our immediate program for victory and peace. But let us not stop there. Let us make clear to our fellow Americans and the whole world that we stand for a continuing program of peace through strength and honor. It is essential that our allies carry more of the load of combatting Communist aggression.

We must insist that they devote more of their manpower and resources. There must be less sitting on the bench. Let us use in this struggle not only the Chinese Nationalists, but other people willing to stand up with us. In Europe there are those ready to help us strengthen the Atlantic Pact and prevent the threats of Soviet aggression breaking into active war. Let us call to our banners the military forces of Spain, of Greece, and of Turkey. Let us use any willing to stand with us and furnish troops. And remember--those troops will take the places of boys we are forced now to draft and send to fight on foreign soil.

America's long-range program should include the strengthening of collective security. To accomplish this, we should vigorously advocate reforming the United Nations. We should make it an organization truly capable of preserving the peace. We must give it the power to define and prevent aggression before armed conflict starts.

Let us revive again those great moral and spiritual values that made and preserved us a great Nation. When Abraham Lincoln said, 'This country cannot exist half slave and half free,' he turned his back upon fear and compromise and took up the torch of freedom and unity. Let our government be courageous enough. 'This world cannot exist in peace and justice half slave and half free. We are determined that all people shall someday be free.'

Let us be courageous enough to declare that it is our purpose to work for a world in which there shall be no more concentration camps with their torture and death, that our crusade shall never end until mankind is blessed with those inalienable rights for which our forefathers fought and died. I say to you that the whole world is waiting for firm, intelligent, and vigorous leadership. With the principles that our nation has espoused since its beginning, with a program to fit the needs of this modern day, and with the election of candidates who will stand fearlessly

CHAPTER 19   THE KOREAN WAR

for what is right, we can give the people of the entire world the leadership they need.[6]

The jeep General Ridgway was driving got too close to the fighting, and a shell blew out the windshield. Ridgway hustled the Congressmen out of the line of fire.

Ms. Sirianni's thesis includes the following: "Armstrong believed that President Truman would secretly offer the island of Formosa, now Taiwan, to China, and the United States would withdraw support (to end the war). In 1951, Formosa was governed under the Constitution of the Republic of China by President Chiang- Kai-shek. To make it difficult for President Truman to offer such a concession, Armstrong called a press conference in Korea and announced that 'the rumors about the United States giving up Formosa were all lies. The United States would never do such a thing.' This stirred up the press corps. The State Department had to deny that there was such a plan."

O. K. continues: "We talked to American officers and enlisted men, who confirmed what we suspected, that the policy of the United States government under Acheson, and of course under Truman, was to simply hold the Communists, not to defeat them --the first non-victory war policy in American history. Well, anyhow, we spent about two weeks over South Korea. We got up to the Hahn River, the border with North Korea. While interviewing General Ridgway I asked him this question: 'Can we win this war fighting it under the handicaps imposed on our forces by the United States government? And he said, 'Positively no.' The handicaps were the following that they would not permit the U.S. army, when they permit our planes to fly to where they could hit the air fields

---

[6] Congressional Record 4812 and 953695

and ammunition depots either in North Korea or in Manchuria. It was a dastardly way to fight a war, compelling our men to fight with one hand tied behind them.

The Acheson policy, adopted soon after World War II, was simply to hold the enemy--don't try to win. After Dorn and I had seen all we needed to see, we went in with Gen. Stratemeyer and Brigadier Gen. Nuckles, who handled publicity for the Air Force. We wanted to see General MacArthur. MacArthur had heard of me through an article I wrote about his fleeing with his wife from the Philippines to Australia and vowing, 'I shall return.'

"MacArthur pointed out to Dorn and me a picture of his wife on the wall and said, 'That's my boss.' We all smiled at that. Now, we learned very quickly from MacArthur that he was under severe pressure. He felt that it was unfair to be restricted in what he was trying to do. He had written a letter to one of the Republican leaders in Congress, Minority leader Martin of Massachusetts, who had written the General to ask, 'Will you tell me how the war is going?' MacArthur expressed himself to Martin as dissatisfied with the Defense Department and with the way the war was going. That letter, unfortunately, hit the newspapers because Congressman Martin released it. That aroused considerable criticism of MacArthur. Now, while I was sitting next to MacArthur conferring on a plan to pull this thing out, he smacked my leg with the back of his hand and said, "After General Stratemeyer briefs you, I want you Congressmen to go down to Formosa--he called it Formosa; He meant Taiwan, of course, although Formosa had been the Portuguese name for Taiwan. It had been owned by the Japanese for half a century. Then after the war they lost it to the victors. In any case, he said, 'I want you to go down

CHAPTER 19   THE KOREAN WAR

there, and I want you to learn a plan we have approved.' Dorn said, 'I'm sorry General, I have to get back to South Carolina for an engagement, and then back to Washington?' Now, our leave of about three weeks was about to expire, but in spite of that I said, 'General, I'll go to Formosa and confer with your men on this plan'. And he said 'Excellent.'

I was immediately ushered into the office of General Stratemeyer. He had a map as big as the whole wall of Japan, Korea and Manchuria. He took a pointer and said, 'We know the location of every airfield and ammunition dump; We know everything about the enemy in North Korea and in Manchuria. There are five roads coming into the Manchuria capital. We know where they are. We could blast them out, and that's what we ought to do. The plan is to utilize Chiang Kai-shek's army. We should have been doing this all along.' Bear in mind, Chiang had been forced out of China in 1949, two years before. But his army was still intact, totaling 450,000 men just waiting and loafing around in Taiwan. Stratemeyer went on: 'General MacArthur has agreed that Chiang Kai-shek will divide those troops. One half of the units will be deployed to Korea.' That would be Asians fighting against Asians, which we didn't have. They were depending on America and British and Turks, Australians, and few other of the allies. General MacArthur and the commanders of the Chinese would plan strategy in Korea. Stratemeyer: 'The other half would make a diversion against mainland China, and that would make a pincher movement'. I am firmly convinced that Red China would have fallen. I

General Chennault

don't think they could have withstood a pincher, a simultaneous movement, from Korea and from the mainland, starting from the Pescadores Islands off the coast of Taiwan. We would have had to furnish the equipment they needed, but they would have made a landing, and I think it would have succeeded, especially with U.S. Air Force cover, including what the Air Force needed to do in Manchuria. So, I said, 'I will go to Formosa.'

I cast around to find a regularly scheduled airline only to find none. But there were occasional flights by Major General Claire Chennault. Gen. Chennault, who had been in World War I, had helped with victory in the far east. He had married a Chinese and had considerable clout with those who knew aviation in the far east.

Before I left, they had a reception for Army Secretary Pace there in Tokyo. I went to that reception. That was on Monday night. I went to Secretary Pace and said to him, "I've been concerned about the criticism that I've read about from Washington. Senator Kerr of Oklahoma has criticized General MacArthur, saying maybe it's time to re-evaluate General McArthur's leadership. These criticisms were based on Acheson's opposition to MacArthur's wanting to win the war in Korea. Secretary Pace said to me, 'Well, don't worry about anything that Senator Kerr might say. I know there is some friction about General MacArthur, but if there were anything of merit in any of these criticisms, I'd know all about it.' This was on Monday night, two days before MacArthur was discharged. At any rate, I found that a military plane was leaving for Taiwan early evening, and so I asked one of the pilots if I could book passage, so to speak. He said, 'We don't have any passenger flights, but we'll be glad to put a chair on one of our freight flights and we'll fly you

CHAPTER 19   THE KOREAN WAR

down there.' Well, it was unheated, and it was cool weather and nearly froze. We stopped in Okinawa where I warmed up, as did the pilots and the sergeant accompanying us.

Just before dawn we reached the airfield at Taipei. I looked out of the window, and in the early morning light I could see that Gen. Chennault had come down to meet me, as had the Assistant Ambassador with a contingent of three or four Americans. One of those fellows grabbed me and took me to a hotel up on a high hill in Taipei, the Grand Hotel, and there I opened my suitcase and was about to crawl into bed for some sleep when the phone rang, and it was this Assistant ambassador. He said, 'Well Congressman, my mistake. The Chinese say they also have a Blair House (President Truman was at the time residing at the Blair House during White House renovations), and it's ready for you. The reason the Chinese officials didn't meet the plane was that I could not convince them that a Congressman would fly on a freight plane. They are acutely embarrassed, their faces are red, and they are coming to get you. So I got dressed quickly, and here came a car with one of the biggest Chinese I ever saw, a Lt. General; I used to know his name very well.

Chiang Kai-shek

He said, 'We have a Blair House, and you're supposed to come and stay with us. The General has ordered it.' Well, there we went. And that house, I learned, had been the Emperor's headquarters every time he came down from Japan during the fifty years that they owned Taiwan, and Okinawa, incidentally. But anyhow, they had a press conference set up for the next afternoon. That night I was entertained by the (sounds like) 'Newan,' they called it, the parliament of the Free Chinese. The next day I attended the press conference at 3 o'clock.

Incidentally, present there were several Chinese graduates of the University of Missouri School of Journalism. They had scattered all over the far east, and I recalled that there were several Chinese students at the University of Missouri School of Journalism when I was a student there. I stood up to speak and had barely introduced myself when the door in the back opened and a Chinese messenger came trotting up the aisle and handed the chairman a telegram. The chairman read it and simply handed it to me. It said, 'President Truman has fired General MacArthur.' I looked at that telegram, and I said, 'Now gentlemen, this is sad news, and I can't believe it. I don't believe that a president would discharge a general as important as MacArthur without a hearing, with no pre-notification of it whatever.'

Madam Chiang Kai-shek

Everybody scattered to scout out any later news. I had dinner that night with Chiang Kai-shek and his aids. The vice president was there, his chief of military staff and one other general. I sat next to Madam Chiang Kai-shek opposite 'the Old Man.'

Chiang was shocked at the news about MacArthur. He kept asking me questions. 'Does this mean you have abandoned us?' 'No, I can't believe that. I think that the American people still wish you well and want to go ahead and win this war in Korea', and so on. He asked several other

CHAPTER 19   THE KOREAN WAR

questions, and then, 'Does this mean that your government has adopted the British plan?' Well, I knew enough about the British plan to answer, but I thought best to hedge by saying, 'I don't believe America will ever adopt a plan of no victory.'

General Douglas MacArthur

I stayed there another two days, doing the best I could to assure the American embassy that, while I didn't know enough about the firing of General MacArthur, I hoped to go back to Tokyo and learn more and find out if I could be of any help to the general. When I got back to Tokyo, General MacArthur was already on his way back to Washington. So, I just took the next plane on back home to Washington myself. Now, General MacArthur came to Washington. He had shucked off his uniform and was in civilian clothes. He addressed a joint meeting of Congress. I think when the great speeches of American history are compiled, that speech will be among them. I saw men sit there and cry when he spoke. He told about how he had tried to uphold the honor and security of America.

The only insubordination even cited by President Truman was that he answered Congressman Martin's letter without going through channels, which meant the War Department and the President of the United States. They never could find any order that he disobeyed because he never disobeyed any. He simply was wedded to the idea that 'We must fight this war to win it,' a predisposition contrary to the Acheson plan. Now, I did some inquiring when I got back to Washington. And the nearest I could learn was that Acheson had decided that the time had come for him to convince Mr. Truman that MacArthur had been disloyal or had disobeyed, or whatever it took. But at any rate, it was said that they held a midnight meeting at the White House, Acheson and several others of the clique around Acheson. Now I can't prove this, but I suspect enough drinks were had by all so that Acheson could effectively say, 'Well, fire the son of a bitch!' and Truman replied, 'Well, I guess I will.' That was 1 am, 3 pm Taiwan time, the very time I was preparing to speak to the reporters in Taiwan.

About two weeks after O. K.'s return from the Far East, General MacArthur's gave his Old-Soldiers-Never-Die valediction. MacArthur's dismissal was the end of any end-the-war plan. A half century later American troops are still sentry in Korea. O.K.'s summary comment on MacArthur's role in the Pacific phase of World War II represents faithfully his regard for the general: "After his dismissal, General MacArthur made no public mention of what should have been done in Korea because there was nothing he could do about it; that was a closed chapter. He did confine himself to a plea that he be recognized for doing his best. And believe me, he deserved credit for winning the war in the Far East, the Pacific. I doubt very much that the war in Europe could have been brought to the speedy conclusion it was without the victory in the Far East. That was to the credit of MacArthur. Of course, there are critics who say that he loved power. Well shucks, so did every other great general who accomplished anything.'"

CHAPTER 20

THE COLD WAR

"The United States must now take a firm stand upon principle in the cold war against communism. The new policy of liberation for the peoples now enslaved by the Soviet Union could prove as far-reaching in its effects as did the Monroe Doctrine in its day. Its implementation by America and our allies would send a wave of hope and faith among peoples behind the Iron Curtain. The aim of liberating captive peoples emphatically does not mean plunging the world into another major war. If the internal resistance of these peoples to communist control is encouraged and properly utilized by the free nations, it will add up to such strength that Stalin and his Kremlin tyrants will not dare launch all-out war. It will mean that we shall have a bold new program dedicated to replacing totalitarian tyranny with free and democratic regimes throughout the world.

If we continue to follow the futile policy of attempting to 'contain' communism in areas it now enslaves, the Soviet masters will continue to digest their gains, liquidate all free elements and gather strength for more attacks upon free peoples."

"Therefore, the policy of liberation can mean the difference between constant aggression and war. The very weapons used by the communists to destroy our resources and liberties; or a lasting peace, based on human rights, equality and justice. We in Congress, of both parties, who have supported a policy of liberation, hope that it will be based on the following:

CHAPTER 20   THE COLD WAR

1. There must never be any compromise with aggression. We should make it clear at once that we will never permit forced repatriation of prisoners of war; we will never admit Red China into the United Nations; and that we will never cease our efforts for a unified, independent Korea.

2. A strong general foreign policy, casting aside all the tragic agreements such as those of Yalta and Potsdam that hinder freedom and peace.

3. Improving and strengthening the United Nations as an instrument for preventing aggression and war and as a more effective agency to combat the world-wide communist conspiracy.

4. Strengthening of resistance movements within the Soviet orbit to bring about corresponding weakening of totalitarian grip.

5. A vigorous program of truth, which will constantly counteract the false propaganda of the Communist regime.

If we are to win the Cold War, we should seize the initiative for peace. The communists have appropriated the very word "peace." Yet their idea of peace is submission to their slave regime. We should convince the world that we of the Free World are ready to join in the inspection and control of all armaments, and only the aggression of the communists prevents this step. We should take the initiative for peace by offering just treaties of peace to Austria and Germany.

We should launch a great propaganda initiative that should be built around a crusade of truth to counteract the lying propaganda of the communists. It should include a campaign of liberation, which will give hope to those behind the Iron Curtain that someday they shall be liberated. It should call for desertions from the Red Army and from all the satellite forces.

We should utilize all our allies willing to stand with us in the Cold War. In the far east, we should enlist the Chinese Nationalists and the guerrillas on the mainland; we should set free all Korean prisoners and permit those who desire to fight for the liberation of their homeland to do so. In Europe, we should enlist the strength of a new and democratic Germany to stand against the Soviet threat.

Finally, we should revive the moral and spiritual strength of this nation so that its leadership may be effective. If these moves are made quickly enough, the Moscow rulers will not be able to take the offensive again.

We can win the Cold War and thus prevent a shooting war. And we can go from there to build a just and lasting peace."

And in a speech to the Women's City Club of Washington and submitted to the press on March 8, 1953, Armstrong said: "In this period of uncertainty caused by Stalin's death, the United States government and people should move quickly into a crusade of psychological strategy to win the Cold War against communism.

Stalin's name struck terror in the hearts of millions the world over. He is the last link to Lenin and the original Bolshevik regime. His successor will not have that advantage -a fact we should capitalize upon at once. An all-out offensive to win the minds and allegiance of peoples now dominated by the late Communist dictator's regime would prevent the outbreak of another war and lead to the downfall of Communism all over the world.

Malenkov and his fellow tyrants in the Soviet Politburo are more afraid of internal resistance on the part of the people now enslaved by the communist regime than they are of all the military weapons of the

CHAPTER 20   THE COLD WAR

free world. If we people of the free world take advantage of the burning desire of these people for their independence, we can drain away Communist strength to such a point that the Red regimes can someday be overthrown.

The first task of our psychological crusade must be to win --and thus end-- the war in Korea. Up to now, because of what General James A. Van Fleet has called the 'sit-down tactics of our own choosing,' we have lost the Korean War. In the eyes of millions of the Far East, the United States and our allies have not been able to make good on our promises to run the aggressors out of Korea and unify the country in peace and freedom. Having disposed of that hot war, we can move to win the Cold War, and thus prevent further aggression on the part of the late tyrant's followers by a program which includes the following items:

1. Liberation for all enslaved peoples. This emphatically does not mean the encouragement of 'Titoism' among the satellites. Breaking away from Moscow is not enough. Communism, with its death to liberty and justice, is the enemy of mankind and not any one regime. Nothing short of replacing communism with liberty and freedom will ensure peace on earth.

2. We must take the initiative for peace. The best place to start would be to write treaties of peace with Germany and Austria, regardless of what the new Russian dictators do. It is nearly eight years since the close of World War II and still no treaties of peace. By this move, we could put a new and democratic Germany in her rightful role as the keystone of peace in Europe.

3. We must move to cut off trade in war materials with the Soviet Union and all her satellites, and if they do not consent to help establish peace, we must cut off all diplomatic relations with them. It is of the

utmost importance that we should make clear to the captive peoples that we do not accept their captivity as a permanent fact of history. This is the new policy of liberation, which will give hope to all peoples behind the Iron Curtain that someday they too may be free."

On Nov. 29, 1953, O. K. took part in a panel discussion of "Freedom and Peace through Liberation" on The Georgetown University Forum. Appearing also were other leaders in the movement, including Michael A. Feighan, Congressman from Illinois; James D. Atkinson, PhD., Head of the Department of Political Science, Georgetown University; and Dr. Slobodan Draskovich, author, lecturer, and the former member of the Institute of National Defense, Yugoslavia. The narrator was Mr. Matthew Warren. The evening`s discussion included these points:

Mr. Warren: "Congressman Armstrong, I would like to ask you first if you would define the term 'Liberation'."

Congressman Armstrong: "Mr. Warren, I believe the term 'Liberation' can be defined as a policy that holds that the people now enslaved by the communist regimes, wherever they may be, are not represented by those regimes rightfully, that those regimes have taken away their liberties and that our policy of liberation holds that we should advise those people in gaining their freedom and establishing democratic governments.

Dr. Draskovich: "Congressman Armstrong, do you mean in the same sense that America has treated Japan and Germany-helping them to help themselves?"

CHAPTER 20   THE COLD WAR

Mr. Armstrong: "Precisely, a good comparison in that our aim is to support those who have been devastated by totalitarianism or are now being oppressed by it."

Mr. Warren: "Dr. Draskovich, could you elaborate on the significance of the title of your policy?"

Dr. Draskovich: "Yes, Mr. Warren. I believe the title is justified for the simple reason that there cannot be peace without freedom. We are facing a highly dynamic hour with an ideology, from Marx to Malenkov, from 1917 and, especially, from the end of World War II, of global domination. In view of the progress of communication and in terms of human and political relations, the world has never been so small as it is today. It is too small for both freedom and slavery. So one or the other has to win, which means that unless communism is destroyed, there can be no peace in the world."

Congressman Feighan: "Mr. Warren, may I add that everyone who seeks freedom will accept help from wherever they can. There is a wonderful exhibition of that when the Nazis went into the Ukraine, the Ukrainians were looking for freedom, liberation and an opportunity to resurrect their own government. Of course, they were fooled by the Nazis and went back with the communists because they were forced to do so."

Mr. Warren: "Dr. Atkinson, the Soviets express an interest in 'co-existence.' What would you say about co-existence?"

Dr. Atkinson: "The term 'co-existence' itself is a Soviet term used especially by Stalin and Malenkov. It has been used by them very cleverly when they want to reassure the Western World just as perhaps a gangster uses soft language in order to assure a future victim. Let us think perhaps of Emerson's statement, 'What you say speaks so loudly that I cannot hear a thing you say'."

Dr. Atkinson: "May I say, in reference to terms such as co-existence and aggression, their use illustrates the tendency of the communists to use our own language to defeat us. As for 'aggressions', in 1940 when the Soviets invaded Finland, they charged that Finland had committed aggression against the Soviet Union.

Again in 1950 when you have the invasion of South Korea by the North Koreans. This was trumpeted all over the world and is being trumpeted at the present time as an invasion of North Korea by South Korea.

That lie is being repeated by Soviet Ambassador Vishinki in the United Nations and by every Soviet propagandist throughout the world. So, no matter what we do, they are going to say it is aggression. That is a constant cover-up for their own aggression."

Congressman Feighan: "We should attack this problem in a two-fold manner: First, by arming ourselves and the free nations of the world to such a military state that war would be prohibitive to any aggressor. In addition to that, we have to let the subjugated peoples realize that the forces of the free world are in their corner. Those forces should be brought vividly to bear in the fact that we, the free people of the world, are advocates of religion, enlightened nationalism, free labor, private property and enterprise."

Congressman Armstrong: "May I pick up this phrase that Congressman Feighan so well used here? That is, the forces of the free world. I would go a step further and say that in my opinion if this policy, this ideal of liberating the people behind the Iron Curtain is carried

CHAPTER 20　　THE COLD WAR

forward by this new Eisenhower administration and by members of Congress united in a bipartisan manner, it will be a deterrent to war instead of provoking war with the Soviet Union. They will see these forces of the free world united in such strength that they will not dare attack. I would like to point out also that our ideal of liberation rests on moral principles. As you have said, Doctor, 'This world cannot exist half-slave and half-free'."

Dr. Draskovich: "A great majority of the people behind the Iron Curtain are our allies, allies of the free world. There are six hundred million people who have been enslaved since 1945. If we don't do anything about it, those people who are idealists, who have fought, who are fighting, as we have been in Berlin and Czechoslovakia will stay enslaved.

Poland-- very recently, we have seen the wonderful example of the former prisoners of war in Panmunjom-and so on. Those people who believe in freedom, if their slavery lasts very long and the free world doesn't help them, they will lose faith in us.

To believe that our refusal to accept their dictatorship means war is to ignore the interrelationships between war and policy. Remember that Clausewitz, the well-known strategist, said that war is nothing but the continuation of policy by other means. The Soviets have reversed the order, and for them policy is nothing but unceasing war against us. To embrace the policy of liberation is not to provoke war but only to answer the aggressions of the communists."

Mr. Warren: "Congressman Feighan, besides a strong defense, what other tools are there to implement effectively this policy of liberation?"

Mr. Feighan: "Psychological strategy. We have been on the defensive. We the people of America and the peoples of the free world generally have been on the defensive in the psychological struggle with communist regimes. The crusade for liberation, for freedom, is for the minds and hearts and the allegiances of the people. We should use broadcasts to the fullest measure, even though we have difficulty with the jamming of our programs."

Dr. Draskovich: "Pertaining to the question of liberation is the unfortunate experience of the enslaved peoples during and immediately after the Second World War. They fought valiantly during the war. I remind you of the Warsaw uprising and the struggle and the participation of the Polish troops in the liberation of Italy and the struggle of the national guerrillas of General Mikhailovich and so on. All these people were deceived, they were let down and their communist counterparts were helped. Then, if we think of the conferences of Yalta and Tehran and Potsdam, we realize that we need quite a strong action in order to restore the faith in America of those peoples. Because as things now stand, it is not enough to tell them, 'We haven't forgotten you.' They already know that the United States wants to help them to run their own affairs and to establish an order that corresponds to their situation and to their needs. Successful propaganda can only be part of a successful policy. If the free world limits itself to saying, 'Well, we morally disapprove of your slavery' and do no more, it won't work. The oppressed peoples must see that the propaganda of the West is a supplement to a policy of liberation. Active political warfare has to be carried out in the territory of the communists. By 'active political warfare' I am referring to people who are willing to live and die for freedom. Those people from Romania, Poland, and so on are willing to return there and do anything necessary for the liberation of their people. They will have the support of at least 95 percent of the population that now is oppressed by communism."

Mr. Warren: "Congressman Armstrong, what else can we do?"

Mr. Armstrong: "Behind the iron curtain, in every country there is a well-defined, well-organized underground movement. We should assist the members of that underground movement in their resistance to the communist regime. This phase of our strategy would be coordinated with political-psychological action. I would like to ask Dr. Draskovich, what would you think of the formation of what we might call an army of liberation, to be part of the European Defense Force, made up of such men as General Anders of the Polish Force, refugees and those who escape from behind the Iron Curtain who are willing to join the defense, not simply of the West, but of the entire free world?"

Dr. Draskovich: "I am definitely in favor of that. Their work would come in a final phase after that of those who would subvert from the underground as mentioned by Congressman Armstrong. So that when the armies come, more than half the work would already be done."

Mr. Warren: "Dr. Atkinson, do you really believe now that it is impossible for the Free World to live side by side with communist imperialism?"

Dr. Atkinson: "To answer that, we must consider the writings of Lenin and Stalin's interpretation of Lenin. As well as Stalin's own statements of policy and study what Soviet chief Malenkov said to the 19th party congress in October of just a year ago. Add to all that theory the past 17 years of Soviet practice, then we see that while they may occasionally toss out a few goodies, a few crumbs in the hope that they can buy a certain amount of necessary time, that is when we see those tactical things for what they are. I can see as the only answer in the long run, no. We cannot live with it."

Mr. Warren: "Gentlemen, thank you. Ladies and gentlemen, you have attended the weekly discussion program of the Georgetown Radio Forum, broadcast of which was transcribed in the Raymond Reiss Studio on the campus of historic Georgetown University in Washington D.C."

CHAPTER 21

A SLAP AT THE SOVIETS

If anything, O. K. was not shy as a freshman Congressman. In Sept. 1951, he attended a diplomatic conference in San Francisco for the formal receiving, by the Allied Powers, of the treaty with Japan. All of the top diplomats of the Allied Powers were present.

Armstrong and Gromyko

Kay Armstrong recalled that his dad made quite a commotion at the conference. According to Kay, "During the conference, my dad tipped off the TV cameramen and reporters, telling them to focus on the Soviet Foreign Minister, Andrei Gromyko and one of his advisors, Sergie A. Golunsky. The two Soviets seated themselves at seats on the aisle at the beginning of the conference. Dad (Congressman Armstrong) walked up to Gromyko with a big smile on his face and said, 'I bring greetings from the peace-loving people of the United States.' Gromyko responded with a smile and handshake while the cameras rolled. Then Dad unfolded a map he had previously obtained from the AFL-CIO and said, 'I present you with a map detailing every slave labor camp and gulag now in operation in the Soviet Union.'

The visit jolted the Foreign Minister as he glanced at the map of the gulag just long enough to verify what he had heard, and with photographers' bulbs flashing, crunched it up and dashed it to the floor. Dad picked it up, turned it over, and announced, 'On the reverse side is an account of the population of each slave camp and deaths to date.' Each camp and gulag was marked with the Soviet hammer and sickle. He then handed the map back to Gromyko. Gromyko's composure changed from 'delighted to meet a comrade to a scowl'. Gromyko's aide, realizing how agitated his boss was, took it upon himself to grab the map and hide it while Dad and Gromyko scowled at each other."

It's important to know that the motto of the State of Missouri is "Show Me." The next morning, the *Chicago Tribune* ran a top of first page headline: "Missouri Man Shows Gromyko," with the picture of O. K. presenting his gift to the Soviet minister and another a few seconds later of the disgruntled face of Gromyko.

On Oct. 5, 1951 O. K. made the following remarks to the House of Representatives: "Mr. Andrei Gromyko, chief Soviet delegate, came to disrupt the conference, to delay its proceedings, to divide its delegates into waning factions. They sought to block any effective action by peace-loving peoples to create... peace with Japan. I presented a map of Russia to Gromyko, showing the Soviet slave labor camps, but he would not comment. What comment could he have had? He had been hit by the strongest weapon in the hands of free peoples --the truth. Confronted firmly and relentlessly with the truth, the lying propaganda of Communism falls flat on its face."[7]

---

[7] Congressional Record 12726

During his freshman term in Congress O. K. was voted "Outstanding Freshman" by his House colleagues, notwithstanding his being a minority member. One of life's surpassing perplexities is that such a leader could have failed more than once to take the tide at its flood. During his first term, a new census dictated a redrawing of congressional districts. The new plan combined O. K.'s with that of a Congressman who had served for decades and had spent too much time at happy hour. For reasons far too detailed for this story, O. K. put his sights on other things and decided against opposing the inebriant incumbent in the primary. In September, the family moved back to Springfield, their mid-west home town, a more central location for his continuing career with the *Reader's Digest*. But O. K. would still maintain a presence.

Attempting to hearken back to the town meetings of yore, America's Town Meeting of the Air was a public affairs radio broadcast and one of radio's first talk shows. Beginning as an experiment by the National Broadcasting Company, the program had a discussion format that tried to interest the public in current events and ran from 1935 to 1956. Providing a venue for opposing viewpoints, the program's goal was to create a new kind of educational program that was entertaining and intellectually stimulating. It's well-known guests were experts on the topic of the broadcast and the audience was encouraged to participate. O. K. Armstrong would be one of those guests. In 1952 America's Town Meeting of the Air made its way to Wheaton College. The topic of the broadcast was "What is the answer for Korea" and Dr. Orville

Hitchcock of the University of Iowa served as the moderator for the meeting.

America's Town Meeting of the Air at Wheaton College in 1952

FAIR USE: Its inclusion in the article adds significantly to the article because the photo and its historical significance are the object of discussion in the article.

Dr. You Chan Yang, South Korean Ambassador to United States, Mr. Walter O'Hearn and O. K. represented the various positions. Mr. O'Hearn was executive editor of the Montreal Star and represented the "left" position, while O.K., who also served on the editorial board of Reader's Digest, represented the "right." [Of course he did.]

CHAPTER 22

FAMILY COMPLEXITIES

The following is Charles Armstrong's take on the relationship of his father and stepmother. "Within a few years, O. K. and Marjorie's marriage grew troubled. The boys' early judgment was that Marjorie was the source of conflict. Over the years, that judgement would prove to be an oversimplification. The reason for the change in perspective was the growing recognition that O. K. had a few quirks of his own. A great one is that he was still in love with his first wife, Louise. In conversations with acquaintances and friends, often in Marjorie's presence, O. K. would refer with detectable fondness to 'the children's mother.' Many years after the fact, Marjorie would relate an incident of their engagement. After O. K.'s summertime proposal, Marjorie suggested a certain day in November for their wedding. O. K. was not comfortable with that date since it was too close to the day he and Louise had married. Marjorie then proposed a time later in November. He then, perhaps embarrassed and clearing his throat, specified that as Louise's birthday. Marjorie and O. K. agreed on a day in December.

O. K. Armstrong was not looking for romance, or even love--not this time. He was looking for a problem solver, an organizer. Much later, Kay would tell Charles that as he, O. K. and Milton were walking from their hotel to the church for the wedding, O. K. said: 'Now, believe me, boys, I know what I'm getting into.' Although Marjorie later maintained that she was in love within weeks of the start of their 'courtship,' she must have sensed O. K.'s sentiments to be more pragmatic than romantic. Certainly, she would have preferred romance.

CHAPTER 22 — FAMILY COMPLEXITIES

But she had admired O. K.'s reputation long before she met him, so when the opportunity arose, her thought may have been, 'Better to go for respect and adventure than hold out for a future much less sure.'

Under those circumstances, when Marjorie married O. K., it is not likely that she was not under any illusion about replacing Louise McCool. She said as much a few years into their marriage with a magazine article titled *I Married a Man and Five Children*, wherein she referred to 'my husband's beautiful and beloved first wife.' But what at the outset she had taken as a manageable island loomed increasingly as an archipelago. It would be a most unusual woman, I think, who would find satisfaction in a marriage established on her gifts of order and arrangement. And resentment of a man who tendered her less love than respect must have entered into making their marriage as complex and disconcerting as it was systematized.

When it came to her husband, Marjorie's dealings and sentiments seemed in contention with themselves and with him all too often. Of this duet, number by number, Marjorie seemed to any audience on-first-listening to be the member out of tune. If one steps back to see it, the big picture suggests that the problem was shared. That's a matter of speculation because two material factors are unknowns. One is the degree of O. K.'s honesty with Marjorie about his feelings, which my guess is he expressed less than fully. The other is the question whether Marjorie would have been "this difficult person" had she been happily married? Most of their disagreements impressed me, and I think most bystanders, as reaching for provocation. Except that when O. K. said something that seemed headed for conflict, it often could be somewhat excused as a component of one of his compulsions, such as to save a penny in still another counterproductive way. But Marjorie seemed more consistently game for contention, going a stretch to be at variance with her husband as an almost daily and sometimes hourly ritual.

If the forest of this marriage were a problem for Marjorie, wouldn't it have been more fruitful for her to deal with it than to peck at it tree by tree? She would disagree sensibly when his penny-wise proclivity was sure to be pound foolish. On most other issues Marjorie seemed to turn as if to make sure their purposes would cross. When my brother's divorce gave his ex-wife an opening to change their son's name (born O. K. Armstrong III), Marjorie ordered for her grandson's birthday a plate with the new name and made much ado to her husband of her enthusiasm for this, as if compounding the insult would give her a one-up. And Marjorie would contrive scenes, as if for role-playing. She would repeatedly undercook certain dishes so that O. K. would, again, have to suggest tactfully that 'maybe we should have left it in the oven a little longer.' I always suspected that in this little madness of Marjorie's was method -of which she was at most only vaguely aware-- namely a game of frustration. Her middle name was Competence: if this kitchen number had been anything but a play, she would have had the details nailed on the second or third go, even if cooking was not her idea of recreation.

Even though Marjorie's resentments were bred by her early disillusionment and provoked by continuing frustrations, they always seemed superseded by respect for O. K. and perhaps by her own kind of love (even if not expressed in a manner readily detectable by others). That respect and love engendered a loyalty that seemed to grow paradoxically with her internal conflicts. For example, in O. K.'s absence, or in the one instance of his incapacitation by illness, she was ready with loyal and even devoted leadership. If O. K. was already at the helm during a storm, she served as reliable and efficient mate.

CHAPTER 22 FAMILY COMPLEXITIES

Marjorie was not only full-strength during crises, it seemed as if she got a charge from them. Frustration of being thwarted reached others, and eventually, affected her dealings with everyone she touched. She would obsess over trivia, as whether someone was eating ice cream with too big a spoon. She was not comfortable with young people and had little understanding or tolerance of their shortcomings, a characteristic O. K. attributed to her having had no children of her own. I can hear her exclaiming, 'Small child!' A belittlement she pressed into service occasionally when Stanley or I would do something about as clumsily as expected for a 9 to 14-year-old. Although, words as accurately in conversation as in formal writing, she could be rather blunt, even with friends, associates or acquaintances. This peculiarity considerably chagrinned O. K., who weighed every word before releasing it.

Despite or perhaps because of all this, many adults connected with her personality and found her downright charming. She would pique her husband with points designed to goad, and then weep over him in his absence. Her marriage became an arena in which her devotion and resentment jousted to a draw. An occurrence illustrates devotion on the offense: For some weeks when Charles was 13, O. K. went through his life's worst case of depression. For him, the blues were always situational, and in all but this instance, something to surmount within hours or days. Even when Louise died, he was able to internalize his pain convincingly enough to wage life bearing that cross, heavy to him but barely noticed by others. For O. K., the stress of this occasion weighed close to the burden of the loss of his lover. His Louise's death was a miscarriage of justice, but of such is the Kingdom of Earth. Her death was not at the hands of human villains, whom O. K. had always judged to be subject to the arm of righteousness, provided that arm extended from a straight back. His faith in this code was being challenged as never before. His depression was clinical and had been dragging out for weeks. During this critical interval Marjorie and Charles were driving through the North Carolina mountains toward Ashville. Suddenly she pulled over at an overlook, which Charles took to be the subject for her next photo.

But she led in prayer for O. K. She prayed aloud, trying to blend a theme of *Have Thine Own Way* with tones of petition, consistent with her lifetime credo (All things work together for the good of them that love God, and to them who are called according to His purpose). Her voice showed her credo was now wedged into the straits of the moment." Of the moment Charles would recall, "I could sense the emotional load of this self-baring to the Almighty, its delivery carefully paced so her composure would hold. But in the content and spirit of this prayer, her love --as fierce as it was frustrated for her husband --was as evident as the mountain scene before us."

Kay, O. K., Marjorie, Stanley and Charles circa 1959

[Believed to be 10th Wedding Anniversary in Springfield]

CHAPTER 22   FAMILY COMPLEXITIES

In 1958 Charles Armstrong graduated from Central High School in Springfield, Missouri and started at Wesleyan University in Middletown, Connecticut. During a period of disenchantment at the University he wrote a rambling, disconnected lamentation to his parents in Missouri. O. K. responded with a telegram expressing his understanding and sympathy, although with his implied assumption that Charles would do nothing impetuous such as sharpen a knife or leave school. Marjorie's note was less tactile, observing the aptness of Charles letter for the likes of any psychiatrist with a curious mind. So as team, Marjorie and O. K. were effective since Charles apparently got the message.

CHAPTER 23

FALSELY ACCUSED AND VINDICATION

The prophecies of Dewitt Wallace and Governor Pete Stark had come true. This was the headwaters of O. K.'s bad humor. Wallace had given O. K. and Marjorie a wedding bonus of $5,000, and the Kansas City IRS indicted O. K. for income tax evasion stemming from that gift. They threw in an accusation of tax evasion over a three-year period, 1947-1950, on an amount of income (not amount of tax: amount of income) which had to be less than his lawyer's fee. O. K. wrote to a friend: "You may recall that I am the one whom Governor Stark sent in to help break the Pendergast crowd. They have been after me ever since. They fought me in the legislature; they fought me when I ran for Congress. I was warned that if I ran, my income tax returns would be investigated. A colleague in Congress told me they did him that way. Anyhow, about three weeks ago, one of the D.A.'s assistants phoned my attorney and told him they wish they could get rid of this case; they still do not have the guts to toss it out the window." O. K. was found guilty on tax evasion charges in April 1955. Soon after the trial, seven members of the jury came forth to say that they knew Armstrong was not guilty of fraud; he was guilty only of poor record- keeping (that is, during the years before Marjorie came aboard, after which no more log-keeping negligence).

Three jury members signed affidavits stating that the verdict was a compromise whereby several who declared Armstrong not guilty would agree to vote guilty if the others would recommend leniency. As for

CHAPTER 23   FALSELY ACCUSED AND VINDICATION

those holding out for guilty, there was persuasive evidence that the prosecution was very careful in appointing a political jury.

In a statement to the Springfield News-Leader, O. K. expressed his sentiments: "The bitterest pill in the whole story was being knocked out of public service, in which I hoped to fulfill an ambition to help build world peace. After I left Congress when my district was joined with that of Congressman Dewey Short, I campaigned for General Eisenhower for President. My friend, the late John Foster Dulles, as Secretary of State authorized my appointment as director of public relations for the State Department in March of 1953. Soon after the news of my appointment came out, I was informed that the Kansas City office of the IRS had filed a request for criminal action against me. That ended any appointment."

> In 1963 the U.S. Court of Claims ruled that O. K. Armstrong had never engaged in any fraud. The Court's vindication announcement was 65 pages long. The IRS was ordered to pay back $21,000 to O. K. Early in this story I recognized the moral "Much of what life offers is not due." To paraphrase President Truman: "If you can't stand the heat, stay out of the boiler-room." A crusader's venue is the boiler-room, and there's where O. K. spent his adult life.

It is unclear how O. K. would have done as public relations director for the State Department. That was not his goal. His goal was to use his vision and skills to set the world on a course toward peace, in his view achievable only through world-wide freedom and justice. He knew that if you're going to direct the orchestra you must first secure the baton, at the time in the hand of Mr. Dulles. O. K.'s regard for Mr. Dulles was greater as a friend than as a Secretary of State. He looked upon Eisenhower and Dulles as weak, indecisive and irresolute, not up to dealing with the Machiavellian wiles of Sino-Soviet totalitarianism. He saw the Kremlin oligarchy as a shell that could be cracked with cunning diplomacy and psychological warfare. From the beginning of the Cold War, O. K. had seen the Kremlin bosses as canny men of realism, who knew they would lose all in a confrontation with U.S. power. He became virtually sick with disgust and frustration when the uprising of June 17, 1953 in Germany and the 1956 revolution in Hungary found Eisenhower and Dulles passive. In O. K.'s words: "There we missed two rich opportunities to liberate eastern Europe."

CHAPTER 24

EVANGELICAL CRUSADER

O. K. Armstrong was raised as a fundamentalist Southern Baptist. An active Baptist layman, he maintained a wide circle of contacts in the Protestant world, including the Reverend Billy Graham, Harold Fey, editor of the Christian Century and Glenn Everett of the Religion News Service. His frequent travels across the country and the globe as well as his brief sojourn in Washington had given him a wide range of acquaintances, while his work as a journalist gave him cover to travel the country with-out raising any particular suspicions. However, he was relentless in the pursuit of what he wanted or what he thought other people needed.

Kay Armstrong recalls that when his father was in Washington, he was involved in some assistance to Billy Graham that has gone unreported. According to Kay, "The Billy Graham Greater Washington Evangelistic Crusade was held from Jan. 13-Feb. 17, 1952. The Billy Graham Crusades were very popular with overflow crowds of orderly and worshipful people every night." This particular event had been underway for a couple of days just up the street from the Capitol at the National Guard Armory. At the time, the executive control of the District of Columbia was managed by a commission consisting of a military general and two political appointees, all appointed by the President. Kay remembers that "Reverend Graham called his dad's office because the Commissioners had notified him that they must shut down the Revival as the crowd size exceeded established limits at the Armory. A meeting was set up immediately, with the three

Commissioners, Reverend Graham and his team, and O. K." According to Kay who was 23 years-old at the time, his dad invited him to sit in on the meeting. Early in the meeting one of the Commissioners asked Reverend Graham, "Are you an Evangelist?" Graham replied in a most gracious way, "I don't know whether or not I am an Evangelist, but I try to do the work of an Evangelist." Kay remembers how impressed he was by the humility of the young preacher.

Then the actual meeting began. The Commissioners explained the established written rules of the Armory, and how any changes would require public hearings, etc., the equivalent of "sorry, our hands are tied." Kay says, "My dad cleared his throat, and began to speak his mind in a subtle manner. 'Now, we don't want to set any precedent here, it wouldn't be right, you know, setting a precedent . . .' The Commissioners started to fidget around in the chairs uncomfortably. The other meeting attendees didn't really understand what my dad was up to. But the Commissioners did. O. K. Armstrong had reminded the Commissioners, all Democrats, that 'the Truman inaugural celebration in that very same Armory just two years earlier had overflowing crowds of cigar-smoking, whiskey-drinking, carousing celebrants. Where was the safety concern then?' Suddenly, the meeting was over. My dad joined the Reverend Graham outside at the curb. Graham asked my dad, 'What just happened?' My dad chuckled, 'They have decided the comparison of the two events would not be very good optics for them if they shut down the Crusade. They decided to delay the hearing on the new occupancy level restrictions for six months or so.' Reverend Graham just shook his head.'"

The 1952 Washington-area Crusade concluded with a peace rally on the east steps of the United States Capitol building. Even that part of the event required some intervening by the Armstrong family on behalf of Crusade. Kay Armstrong recalls that the use of the east steps of the Capitol for a concluding sermon by the Reverend Graham would not be possible since it was not a Federally-authorized event and there may be technical issues. The 23-year-old Kay arranged for Cliff Barrows, the program manager and choir director for the Crusades, and George Beverly Shea, the famous baritone with the Crusades to meet with the Capitol architect to discuss the matter. After some discussion, the architect concluded that there was no technical reason why the steps could not be used. The commissioners must have agreed since permission was granted for the Reverend to preach from the east Capitol steps.

The next day during the rally, Billy Graham took the opportunity to encourage President Truman to establish a National Day of Prayer. It was a historic moment that had an immediate impact. Within two days, legislation was introduced in the House of Representatives and passed after committee action by unanimous vote. President Harry Truman signed the joint resolution into law in April 1952. (Allmond, 2010)

In the 1960s O. K.'s faith beliefs would result in his involvement, if not outright leadership in the Protestant resistance to young, Catholic, war hero, Presidential Candidate, John Fitzgerald Kennedy.

The day before the West Virginia Democratic presidential primary in May 1960, Nixon advisor (and eventual titular campaign manager) Robert Finch gave a brief speech to a group of supporters to outline the strategy for the coming campaign. Nixon's internal polls at that point showed him leading all the possible Democratic nominees except Kennedy, who led Nixon 52% to 48%. The Nixon brain trust did not think that Kennedy would win big in West Virginia. In the unlikely event that he did, there would be no way to prevent Kennedy from winning the nomination. But without a large victory, they felt, the contest would be decided by the convention, and Stevenson would prevail. There would, however, be tremendous pressure for Kennedy to take the second slot. While they thought that Kennedy was the strongest vote-getter among the Democratic candidates, there was no way to know how many Catholic votes he would bring to the Democrats if he ran for vice president with Stevenson or Johnson atop the ticket.

Finch promised that the Nixon campaign would be the most unorthodox in the nation's history. While he did not fully explain what this meant, he did note that Nixon would act as his own de facto campaign manager, consulting periodically with Senator Thruston Morton of Kentucky, chair of the Republican National Committee; Senator Barry Goldwater, chair of the Republican Senatorial Campaign Committee; and Representative William Miller, chair of the Republican Congressional Campaign Committee. Nixon would be his own chief advisor.

So as late as May, the Nixon campaign felt that Kennedy would likely not be at the top of the ticket. While this differs somewhat from Nixon's own analysis well alter the election was over, it helps to account for why they did not have a fully developed strategy for addressing Kennedy's Catholicism. The problem of holding on to Republican Catholics while facilitating a mass defection of Democratic Protestants was a tricky one that they hoped to avoid. When Kennedy did win the West Virginia primary and emerge as the Democratic candidate, the religion issue moved to the forefront for both campaigns.

O. K. would enter the battle. Days before the Republican convention opened in Chicago, he wrote to Albert "A. B." Hermann, a senior official at the Republican National Committee. Hermann would be named national campaign director for the RNC, and he would coordinate the day-to-day activities for the RNC and Nixon headquarters. O. K. outlined a series of steps that the campaign could take in order to exploit Kennedy's Catholicism among a wide range of Protestants. Hermann immediately wrote back and told Armstrong to contact him immediately after the convention. But O. K. could not wait. He phoned Hermann instead and got an employee pass to the convention. On July 16, 1960, a week before the convention, O. K. wrote to Hermann and reported that he was beginning to gather a mass of information on church leaders, meetings, conventions, conferences, and publications, "which will give us a powerful medium of expression." He added, "Perhaps Chairman M. [Morton] would like to glance at it." He also promised to report to Hermann at the convention. On the one hand, his age and his location in Missouri made O. K. a highly unlikely candidate to become the off-the-record organizer of anti-Catholic forces for Nixon. On the other hand, he was the perfect person for the job.

Hired by the Nixon campaign to aid the forces of anti-Catholicism across the country, he could contact the leaders of sympathetic organizations and offer his aid to them without ever having to directly reveal that he was on the payroll of the Republican National Committee. At the age of 66, O. K. had found his highest political calling. In one sense, O. K. had already begun his work for Nixon at the annual meeting of the Southern Baptist Convention in May 1960. On the fourth day of the national meeting, Armstrong helped to pass a resolution that expressed deep reservations about Kennedy's candidacy without ever naming him. This would be a common strategy throughout the campaign. How could they mobilize this grassroots anti-Catholic sentiment?

The way to proceed, O. K. argued, was to contact religious leaders and encourage them to issue statements, print materials, and talk to political leaders in their states who would help to take the lead in spreading the word and influencing the public. The strategy would be to work only with officials and trusted leaders and through them move to community action. With no sense of irony, the man who had helped the Southern Baptist Convention to pass a resolution calling for elected officials to be free of pressure and coercion from religious leaders set out a grand strategy to use religious leaders to build a grassroots campaign to pressure Protestants to vote against a Catholic.

Soon thereafter, Armstrong began to recruit leaders willing to work against Kennedy. A live-page confidential memo outlined the movement's organization and leaders, its plan of action, and its budget." O. K. would coordinate all of the efforts of the disparate Protestant groups working against Kennedy. Since so many churches had expressed misgivings about Kennedy, this coordination could solidify support for religious freedom and for the principle of the separation of church and state, and it could convince church members of the probable weakening of the First Amendment to the Constitution if Kennedy were elected. The campaign would not encourage religious bigotry or make false accusations against the Catl1olic church, but it would encourage factual and dignified discussions by Protestant ministers and church leaders throughout the country. Armstrong had already contacted several outstanding Protestant leaders in order to give proper direction to "our movement." All of them were eager to lend their leadership and their organizations to the work at hand. He claimed that these leaders and their associates were in contact with at least 80% of all the Protestants in the country. While the range of leaders Armstrong would contact was impressive, he was undoubtedly exaggerating his own influence. He was quite careful never to explicitly reveal his formal relationship with the Nixon campaign. But at the same time, the leaders to whom he talked had to know that he had some official sanction, or they would have never given him the level of attention he was able to elicit. (Casey, 2009)

The Reverend Billy Graham sent a letter to the two million people on his mailing list encouraging them to "organize their Sunday school classes and churches to get out the vote." Nixon's support came from an unprecedented ecumenical coalition of religious groups who had never before worked together, but who found common cause ln preventing a Catholic from becoming the nation's next President. "I am convinced at we are involved ln a deep spiritual struggle," Graham said. 'There is an unseen battle wagging that does not show up in the polls and statistics." The Reverend Graham and O.K.'s effort would be unsuccessful. Nixon would lose to Kennedy in a close vote that would be settled by fishy business in the State of Ohio.

Evangelicals were despondent when Nixon lost the election since they had viewed him as their last chance to stop a Catholic onslaught. Weeks after the election, some ministers, such as the Oakland, California Baptist pastor G. Archer Weniger, were still placing their hope in a recount that could swing the election to Nixon. When they finally had to admit defeat, they could scarcely come to terms with the deathblow that they felt the election had rendered to their dream of a Protestant nation. "We have felt like the death of a loved one has taken place-not the death of an individual, but the death throes of a nation," Billy Graham's father-in-law, L. Nelson Bell, said after the election. The country could now expect "a slow, completely integrated and planned attempt to take over our nation for the Roman Catholic Church." But Bell 'praised Nixon for his efforts on behalf of the Protestant cause.

"You, Dick, stood or the things which have made America great, while Mr. Kennedy appealed to the most venal elements in individuals and society as a whole," Bell told Nixon. "I feel that the judgment of God hangs over a people to whom He has given so much and who have rejected spiritual values for those which are material To see out nation in the hands of a conceited, arrogant and inexperienced young man ls a frightening thing. But God may use it yet to bring us to our knees."

CHAPTER 25

O.K.'S POST VIETNAM WAR ANALYSIS

O.K.'s youngest son, Charles, would graduate from Wesleyan then from medical school at the University of Missouri. In the spring of 1968, about two months before the end of his internship at St. Luke's, a letter from the Army appeared with the heading "Welcome to the Vietnam Transient Detachment." Charles older brother Stanley had begun active duty service as an MP in the Army in 1964 just before the Bay of Tonkin incident. Stanley recalls the news from his commander just hours after that precursor to that new war in the Pacific. "Well boys, it seems we have a new enemy. It's called Vietnam or something like that." As luck would have it, Stanley would serve out his enlistment in the States. Perhaps it wasn't luck so much as Stanley would discover that his personnel jacket had PI initialed on the cover. According to Stanley, that meant Political Influence.

Stanley Armstrong 1964

CHAPTER 25 O. K.'S POST VIETNAM WAR ANALYSIS

At the time, O. K. Armstrong, had been an ex-Congressman for some years and was writing full time for the Reader's Digest. "O.K." had given up any hope for sane leadership in the Vietnam War until after the November election. Charles would later relate, "If I had had a crystal ball, I would have warned Dad that the Nixon-Kissinger leadership would be a slight improvement, which is to say highly-disappointing." Charles would serve as a Flight Surgeon in Vietnam.

Cpt. Charles L. Armstrong

Reasonable people debated America's role in Vietnam. President Kennedy promoted "counterinsurgency" as the answer to Communist expansion. After a 1961 meeting with Soviet Premier Nikita Khrushchev in Vienna, Kennedy said, "In the 1940s and early '50s, the greatest danger was from Communist armies marching across free borders, which we saw in Korea. Now we face a new and different threat. The local conflicts they support can turn in their favor through guerrillas or insurgents or subversion." Vietnam, Kennedy said, would be a test case of our resolve to combat that subversion, and he set out to redesign the military for that purpose; The CIA's Douglas Blaufarb, in his 1977 history of the counterinsurgency era, noted that President Kennedy "took the lead in formulating the programs, pushing his own staff and the government establishment to give the matter priority attention." Kennedy fired Army Chief of Staff George Decker for insufficient commitment to counterinsurgency. Kennedy championed the Army Special Forces ("Green Berets") and increased the number of U.S. military advisers in Vietnam from 900 when he took office to 16,300 at the time of his death. Communist insurgents disappeared from battle in Vietnam following their disastrous 1968 Tet Offensive. (South Vietnam was not defeated by guerrilla insurgents but by a massive cross-border World War-II style blitzkrieg of 20 divisions of North Vietnamese regulars in 1975.)

As for the management of the war, for several years O. K. had been tearing out his hair over the Johnson administration's galactic, invincible incompetence. In 1981, he looked back: "Just as Dean Acheson felt that the best policy was to avoid winning and just hold them enough that they'll get discouraged, so Johnson and MacNamara in Vietnam. We mustn't win the war, but we must keep throwing men in there, and that will discourage them.

To O. K. Armstrong civilian control of the military was imperative. On the other hand, any military commander reticent in the face of civilian defeatist policy lethal to American troops and sailors was a servile coward. O. K.'s contempt for waxen soldiers was in direct proportion to their rank. In 1966, in a letter to Richard Nixon, whom he suspected would be the next GOP presidential nominee, O. K. set forth his six-part outline for bringing the war to an end favorable to the Vietnamese people. On the part of the (U.S.) government: 1. Announce

CHAPTER 25   O. K.'S POST VIETNAM WAR ANALYSIS

a clear, easily understood statement of policy... and our determination to restore peace and stability in the area. 2. Stop all weakening statements about negotiations. On the part of the military: 1. Give free rein to the U.S. and Vietnam military forces, working together, to carry out the policy of winning the war quickly. 2. Mine the Harbor of Haiphong and other coastal import centers, notifying all foreign shippers...no more military material...to come to North Vietnam. 3. Bomb the military targets of North Vietnam until all have been systematically destroyed. 4. Permit commanders in the field and on the sea to co-ordinate their strategic and tactical activities. Not included here but a point I heard repeatable from O. K.: If the U.S. Navy and Air Force were allowed a sane military strategy, only minimal, if any, American ground troops would be needed. Nixon wrote back: Dear O. K., (preliminaries; then): "I agree with those who contend that repeated statements of our desire to negotiate weaken our position and only serve to convince the enemy that we desperately want 'out.' An increasing number of Americans have come around to the view that if we are going to fight this war, then let's not fight it by communist rules."

General John K. Singlaub offers the following history: "Communist supplies from China, Russia and East Europe destined for North Vietnamese and Viet Cong forces were being offloaded at the Port of Haiphong and moved through Hanoi to the logistics system which brought them through a network of trails. There was one major railroad that came down from the Quijing area through a gorge. The more significant movement of supplies from China were on a single railroad down from Nanjing connecting to Lang Son (at NE border of North VN and China) and then into Hanoi. We interdicted that, after which they found it easier to move supply ships into the Port of Hai Phong where they had sanctuary, 'they' being the Chinese, the Russians, and the East Europeans. Russia, Poland and Czechoslovakia were much greater sources of supply than China. MACSOG, the Military Assistance Command Studies Operations Group, was a joint Army-Navy unit specializing in clandestine-missions such as assassination and infiltration. For example, MACSCG troops placed ARVN guerrilla forces, customarily 120 indigenous led by 16 Americans, at a key road junction in the north on the Ho Chi Minh Trail up toward the northern border of South Vietnam, just inland. For three days at a time one company would locate and destroy ammo dumps and direct bombing offensives to cut the trail. A company would bivouac at a critical road junction or on land overlooking such a junction where they could call in air strikes day and night. But what we damaged or destroyed the Communists would repair within 24 hours. Operation Tailwind, by infiltrating major North Vietnamese transportation unit headquarters, captured some of the cardinal documents of the war. With this information we could have done much more damage to the Trail, if allowed. Even at that, if we had taken out Hai Phuong, we could have ignored the Trail. A competent plan would have included the elimination of the enemy's supply routes and sources, including his ports, and elimination of his command and control centers and of Chinese rail lines and sanctuaries. MacNamara and Johnson just didn't get it." [end Singlaub].

As for any Chinese troop threat: They were not suited up for the game. The Chinese were in the midst of their Cultural Revolution at the time and had to pull their troops out of Vietnam. They did occupy the northernmost province, Phongsali, of Laos, and they kept advisers with key North Vietnamese units. (Many of these advisers were removed by U.S. Army special-operations troops during the Son Tay raid led by Col. Bull Simon.) The Chinese Communists also had air defense units

CHAPTER 25   O. K.'S POST VIETNAM WAR ANALYSIS

around and north of Hanoi. There were restrictions against attacking those and against going up to the border of China or across the border of Laos.

Marjorie Armstrong's brother, Lt. Gen. Joseph Harold Moore, commanded the U.S. Air Force Pacific-Vietnam theater at the time [under the general Pacific command of Admiral Sharp or McCain or, perhaps, Gen. William C. Westmoreland.] During leave to visit his ailing mother who lived in our home (after O. K. Armstrong had written his letter to Nixon), the Air Force General very clearly outlined measures needed to bring the war to a speedy end, after which a toddler Vietnamese democracy could begin its first steps. In 1981, O. K. remembered: "Now, Marjorie's brother sat on our settee there (pointing), having come all the way from Vietnam to see his ill mother before she died. I said, 'Well General, tell me how we should win that war.' And he said, 'There are three things. In the first place, we should close the passageways open to the Communists coming into South Vietnam. In the next place, we should take out the port of Haiphong. Bear in mind, Russian ships were coming in constantly, and American fliers were not allowed to put a stop to that atrocity--one of the most craven policies ever followed in war. And he said, 'We know where their depots are. We should blast those out. Finally, eliminate all military communication and supply infrastructure, such as rail lines, roads, bridges and ports. The war would be ended in 90 days' time if not before.' Well he was right. These measures would have required few, if any, U.S. ground forces but Vietnamese troops in cooperation with the U.S. Air Force and U.S. Navy. There was no excuse for Johnson's sending half a million men to Vietnam. They were utterly needless; fighting in the jungle on the enemy's terms."

A winning strategy in Vietnam would have pertained in either major phase of the war: during the guerrilla-counterinsurgency phase that ended with the disastrous failure of the enemy's 1968 Tet Offensive, or during the post-Tet North Vietnamese Army phase when the NVA invaded South Vietnam with tanks and artillery. Except that if this win strategy had been operative during the first phase, there would not have been a second phase. By reason of that, my opinion at the time was that we should decide whether or not we belonged in Vietnam. If we did belong, then we should turn the war over to professionals who knew what they were doing. If we had no legitimate role, then pack up and go home.

Meanwhile there was something about the U.S. military leadership that disturbed all troops allied in Vietnam. Junior-officer rank felt free to discuss the matter amongst ourselves. That "something" was the military chiefs' moral deficiency in failing to stand up and inform the American people that a political syphilis had invaded and corrupted the head of the American body politic, and that President Johnson and his band of the best and brightest blockheads and whiskies were conducting one of history's most eminent military, political and moral disasters. From the time Charles was transferred to the Delta, he began to hear, mainly through off-the-cuff remarks, about how the real soldiers of all ranks felt. Infantry soldiers from sergeants to majors related their frustration: "While our huge resources at the depots and stations such as Cam Ran Bay and Ton Son Nhut sprawl unused, we watch a dozen helicopters take off simultaneously to wage another search-and-destroy mission on the enemy's terms."

As 1969 aged, Nixon and Kissinger were giving the impression of having learned nothing and having forgotten nothing. By 1973, all the main combat divisions had pulled out, the South Vietnamese marines and special forces were calling the shots against, and defeating, the

CHAPTER 25   O. K.'S POST VIETNAM WAR ANALYSIS

North Vietnamese. President Thu requested from President Nixon permission to take the war up Highway 1 north against North Vietnam (In 1974, Kissinger vetoed this). Now things were coming unhinged. The Kennedy-Tunney Amendment to the 1975 D.O.D. appropriations bill curtailed ammunition to the Cambodian campaign and was followed hard by Congressional restrictions of assistance to Vietnam's anti-Communists. The Communists knew American resolve was gone and made their plans accordingly.

Again, from O. K.'s 1981 reminiscences: "Let me go back to that Tet Offensive. In the Tet Offensive, the Communists went all out to attack the cities and towns, forty some of them. They thought that the people of Vietnam would rise up and join them. They were mistaken. While they demolished the towns in some areas, none rose up to join the Communists, which should not have surprised anybody. "The Tet Offensive should have been followed by the President of the United States saying, 'Now you are defeated, now you must surrender, and if you don't we'll continue until there is no North Vietnam Army left.'" If he had said that they would have surrendered, and we would have brought that war to an end. But he didn't have the nerve, he didn't have the guts, he didn't have the manhood. Furthermore, if MacArthur had been allowed to win the Korean war, the Vietnam war never would have happened because the Communists would have been broken in the East. In neither war did we do anything we should have done. In Korea we missed a great chance to stamp out Communism in the Far East. Now, some weak-minded people say, "Well, it's a good thing because now (1981) the Chinese are opposing the Soviet Union." There are two faults there: Communist China looks upon us as their enemy, not the Soviet Union, and such people underestimate and misread Communist Chinese intentions.

CHAPTER 26

FINAL COMMENTS

Orland Kay Armstrong was a brilliant and well-educated man. He had many earned academic degrees and would go on to receive many other honorary degrees before he passed away on April 15, 1987, in Springfield, Missouri. He was an often reluctant, but aggressive warrior who sought the Truth, defended Liberty and was a crusader for Peace and champion of the Underdog.

According to his youngest son Charles, "Until his health waned in his 90s, O. K. Armstrong would lead all sizes of crusades, with themes such as integrity vs. governmental corruption; peace-the health of nations and international relations, which he believed to be founded on liberty and justice; and moral strength--to him the rule of the road to be fulfillment in life." (Charles L. Armstrong)

Without the perspective of the written text by O. K.'s son Charles and the transcriptions that Charles made of interviews with his father and of interviews with others that his father conducted, it is doubtful that we would see this side of the man, Orland Kay (O. K.) Armstrong. O. K. was a conservative Christian. It is therefore unlikely that the secular media of today would present his life history in a favorable light. It is strange that the man who was the founding director of the School of Journalism at the University of Florida, who graduated from the University of Missouri at Columbia School of Journalism studying under the distinguished Walter Williams-the originator of the Journalistic Creed-would be so poorly regarded by the mainstream media. Perhaps this book will help that profession make a course correction toward the Truth and, aided by that Creed, refocus on the actual duties of a Free and Fair Press. So, what exactly was that Journalist's Creed?

THE JOURNALIST CREED

"The Journalist's Creed is a personal affirmation of journalism ethics written by Walter Williams in 1914. The creed has been published in more than 100 languages, and a bronze plaque of The Journalist's Creed hangs at the National Press Club in Washington, D.C. Williams was the founding dean of the Missouri School of Journalism." (HEARTLAND REBELLION, 2018, pp. 20-22)

The Creed is as follows:

I believe in the profession of journalism.

I believe that the public journal is a public trust; that all connected with it are, to the full measure of their responsibility, trustees for the public; that acceptance of a lesser service than the public service is betrayal of this trust.

I believe that clear thinking and clear statement, accuracy and fairness are fundamental to good journalism.

I believe that a journalist should write only what he holds in his heart to be true.

I believe that suppression of the news, for any consideration other than the welfare of society, is indefensible.

I believe that no one should write as a journalist what he would not say as a gentleman; that bribery by one's own pocketbook is as much to be avoided as bribery by the pocketbook of another; that individual responsibility may not be escaped by pleading another's instructions or another's dividends.

I believe that advertising, news and editorial columns should alike serve the best interests of readers; that a single standard of helpful truth and cleanness should prevail for all; that the supreme test of good journalism is the measure of its public service.

I believe that the journalism which succeeds best — and best deserves success — fears God and honors Man; is stoutly independent, unmoved by pride of opinion or greed of power, constructive, tolerant but never careless, self-controlled, patient, always respectful of its readers but always unafraid, is quickly indignant at injustice; is unswayed by the appeal of privilege or the clamor of the mob; seeks to give every man a chance and, as far as law and honest wage and recognition of human brotherhood can make it so, an equal chance; is profoundly patriotic while sincerely promoting international good will and cementing world-comradeship; is a journalism of humanity, of and for today's world.

I have reprinted this Creed in several of my books. My hope is that some day it will be re-embraced by the profession of legitimate journalists and the public will once again be served by those dedicated to presenting the truth on matters that effect their very lives.

ABOUT THE AUTHOR

Martin Capages, Jr. is a retired professional engineer, technical executive, and an Army veteran. His technical and management experience includes aircraft design, petroleum exploration and production, computer modeling and technology applications and structural engineering. He began writing political commentary in 2009 and completed his first book, *The Moral Case for American Freedom*, in July 2017. His writing is from the perspective of an engineer, Christian layman, conservative and Constitutional originalist.

Martin attended Missouri State University and the Missouri University of Science and Technology where he graduated with a Bachelor of Science in Mechanical Engineering in 1967. After receiving his Commission as an Army Ordnance Officer but prior to reporting for active duty, he joined Boeing Aircraft in Wichita as an Associate Engineer working on the new 737. He reported for active duty in June 1967. After completing active duty, Martin joined Exxon in Houston, Texas, with assignments throughout the U.S. and Europe to include serving as acting North Sea Development Planning Manager for Exxon in London, Production Operations in the Gulf of Mexico, Engineering Manager for the Texas Midland District, the Alaska Financial and Facilities groups, and Exxon's Western Division Computing organization. He left Exxon in 1984 to join Kerr McGee in Oklahoma as Manager of Engineering Services until 1992 when he left the petroleum industry to start his own structural engineering consulting firm, ARIS Engineering Inc., in Springfield, Missouri. He continued post-graduate studies in Civil Engineering and Management receiving an earned Doctorate in Engineering Management in 2002. He retired from full time practice in 2012.

Martin is married to Pamela Kay Capages. They have five children and seven grandchildren. Both Martin and Pamela are active members of their local Baptist church and serve in other state and international Christian ministries. Pamela is an author in her own right and has published books of poetry concerning her Christian faith, family and personal observations of nature.

DISCLAIMER

This biography has been authorized by the immediate family and heirs of Orland Kay Armstrong, U. S. Congressman from Missouri.. Much of the material is based on the writings of the late Dr. Charles Lindbergh Armstrong published in *A WAKEFUL WATCH* as a posthumous biography. The biographer, Dr. Martin Capages Jr., and publisher, American Freedom Publications LLC, are not offering it as a factual accounting of events.

While best efforts have been used in preparing this book, the biographer and publisher make no representations or warranties of any kind and assume no liabilities of any kind with respect to the accuracy or completeness of the contents and specifically disclaim any personal references to actual individuals mentioned by Dr. Armstrong.

Neither the biographer nor the publisher shall be held liable or responsible to any person or entity with respect to any loss or incidental or consequential damages caused, or alleged to have been caused, directly or indirectly, by the information contained herein.

BIBLIOGRAPHY AND WORKS CITED

Allmond, J. (2010, May 3). *A Legacy of Revival in the Nation's Capital*. Retrieved from billygraham.org: https://billygraham.org/story/a-legacy-of-revival-in-the-nations-capital/

Anadarcia Sirianni. (1992). Orland Kay Armstrong: Writer, Educator, and Public Servant:. *Orland Kay Armstrong: Writer, Educator, and Public Servant: A Thesis Presented to the Graduate Council of the University of Florida in Partial Fulfillment of the Requirements for the Degree of Master of Arts in Mass Communications*. University of Florida .

Capages Jr., M. (2018). *A WAKEFUL WATCH*. Springfield, Missouri: American Freedom Publications LLC.

Capages Jr., M. (2018). *BOOTS TO BOGIES TO BRONZE: The authorized WW11 biography of 2lt Jack C. Pyatt*. Springfield, Missouri: American Freedom Publications LLC.

Capages Jr., M. (2018). *HEARTLAND REBELLION*. Springfield, Missouri: American Freedom Publications LLC.

Casey, S. (2009). *The Making of a Catholic President: Kennedy vs. Nixon 1960*. Oxford University.

Sherman, S. (2011, June 29). *Major Thomas B. McGuire, Jr*. Retrieved from acepilots.com: https://acepilots.com/usaaf_mcguire.html

Williams, D. K., & Gifford, L. J. (2012). *The Right Side of the Sixties: Reeexamining Conservatism's Decade of Transformation*. Springer.

NOTABLE BOOKS

Armstrong, Orland K. *Life and Time of Dr. A. A. Murphree,* Florida: The Record Company, 1928.

Armstrong, Orland K. *Old Massa's People: The Old Slaves Tell Their Story.* Indianapolis: Bobbs-Merrill, 1931.

Armstrong, Orland K. *The Fifteen Most Decisive Battles of the United States.* New York: Longmans, Green and Co.-, Inc., 1961.

Armstrong, Orland K. and Marjorie. *Religion Can Conquer Communism.* Thomas Nelson Sons, 1964.

Armstrong, Orland K. and Marjorie. *The Indomitable Baptists: A Narrative of Their Role in Shaping American History.* Doubleday and Co., 1967.

Armstrong, Orland K. and Marjorie. *Baptists who Shaped a Nation.* Broadman, 1975.

Armstrong, Orland K. and Marjorie. *The Baptists in America.* Doubleday and Co., 1979.

OTHER REFERENCES

Anadarcia Sirianni, was a University of Florida graduate student, completed her 1992 master's thesis titled *Orland Kay Armstrong: Writer, Educator, and Public Servant: A Thesis Presented to the Graduate Council of the University of Florida in Partial Fulfillment of the Requirements for the Degree of Master of Arts in Mass Communications.*

J. M. Roberts CBE was Warden at Merton College, Oxford University, until his retirement and is widely considered one of the leading historians of his era. He is also renowned as the author and presenter of the BBC TV series *The Triumph of the West* (1985) and *The History of the World,* Sixth Edition by J.M. Roberts and O.A. Westad. He died in 2003.

John Kirk Singlaub (born July 10, 1921) is a highly decorated former OSS officer, a founding member of the Central Intelligence Agency (CIA), and a retired Major General in the United States Army. In 1977 Singlaub was relieved from his position as Chief of Staff of U.S. forces in South Korea after criticizing President Jimmy Carter's decision to withdraw U.S. troops from the Korean peninsula in an interview with the *Washington Post.* Less than a year later Singlaub was forced to retire after publicly questioning President Carter's national security policies. In 1979 Singlaub founded the Western Goals Foundation, a private intelligence network that was implicated for supplying weapons to the contras during the Iran-Contra affair. Singlaub has contributed to several books, as well as writing an autobiography.

Harry G. Summers Jr. (May 6, 1932 – November 14, 1999) is best known as the author of the neo-Clausewitzean analysis of the Vietnam

War titled, *On Strategy: A Critical Analysis of the Vietnam War* (1982). Summers was an infantry colonel in the United States Army and had served as a squad leader in the Korean War and as a battalion and corps operations officer in the Vietnam War. Colonel Summers was also an instructor and Distinguished Fellow at the Strategic Studies Institute at the U.S. Army War College in Carlisle, Pennsylvania, and served on the negotiation team for the U.S. at the end of the Vietnam War.

Charles Augustus Lindbergh

https://en.wikipedia.org/wiki/Charles_Lindbergh

Letter from O. K. Armstrong to son Kay

1307 BENTON AVENUE
SPRINGFIELD. MISSOURI

Sunday, April 28, 1946

Dear Kay:

It is Sunday night, and I have been so busy for weeks that I could not write you. At any rate, that is the excuse, and believe me, I've been working night and day on several articles and trying to finish the LeTourneau book. It is almost done. I leave Tuesday for the east, to see the *Digest* crowd and to lay plans for more work. Never a dull moment.

Now, I really got a kick out of the account of your fight with that guy. You did exactly right. Never pick a quarrel or a fight. But if some fellow jumps on you, under the false impression that you are yellow, then give him the works. Some men, unfortunately, can learn no other way. They do not have sense enough to let peaceful men alone, and they mistake other men's peaceful actions for weakness. They have to have sense pounded into them, and the process is painful. I am sure you handled yourself with credit. Keep in good condition, and remember it was Theodore (the Great) Roosevelt who said, "Trust in God and take your own part."

Boy, howdy, everybody has been thrilled over the stuff you've sent back. That last consignment of linens, hand-kerchiefs, etc., was grand. It came while the ladies of the missionary circle were here, and mother displayed the stuff for them. They were google-eyed. The little boys have a fit over it. They took one of the Jap flags to Sunday school this morning, and Charles began waving it in church. It almost broke up the meeting.

I plan to go to the S. Baptist Convention, way down in Miami, Florida. I ought not to take the time but can take a lot of work with me. I want to put through some resolutions. You may have seen my story in the May issue of the *Digest*. I am hearing from it widely.

This afternoon, the Drury band put on a concert of original music from Prof. Rockwell. It was good. Some of it slightly corny, perhaps, but on the whole, he has whipped that Drury band into a good outfit. The other night Mother and I heard the H. S. orchestra. Boy, what an outfit that is No better than when you were there, however. I do want you to get back to the clarinet. By the way, it seems that you may be coming back. Good work! Don't get impatient or worried about it. My guess is that it will be late summer. The longer you stay, the longer your G. I. education. But hurry home soon as possible. I may drop into the Navy in Washington this coming week and ask some of my friends there the lowdown.

Do keep well, and love from all, --Daddy.

Letter from Charles To Kay (with note from Mom Louise)

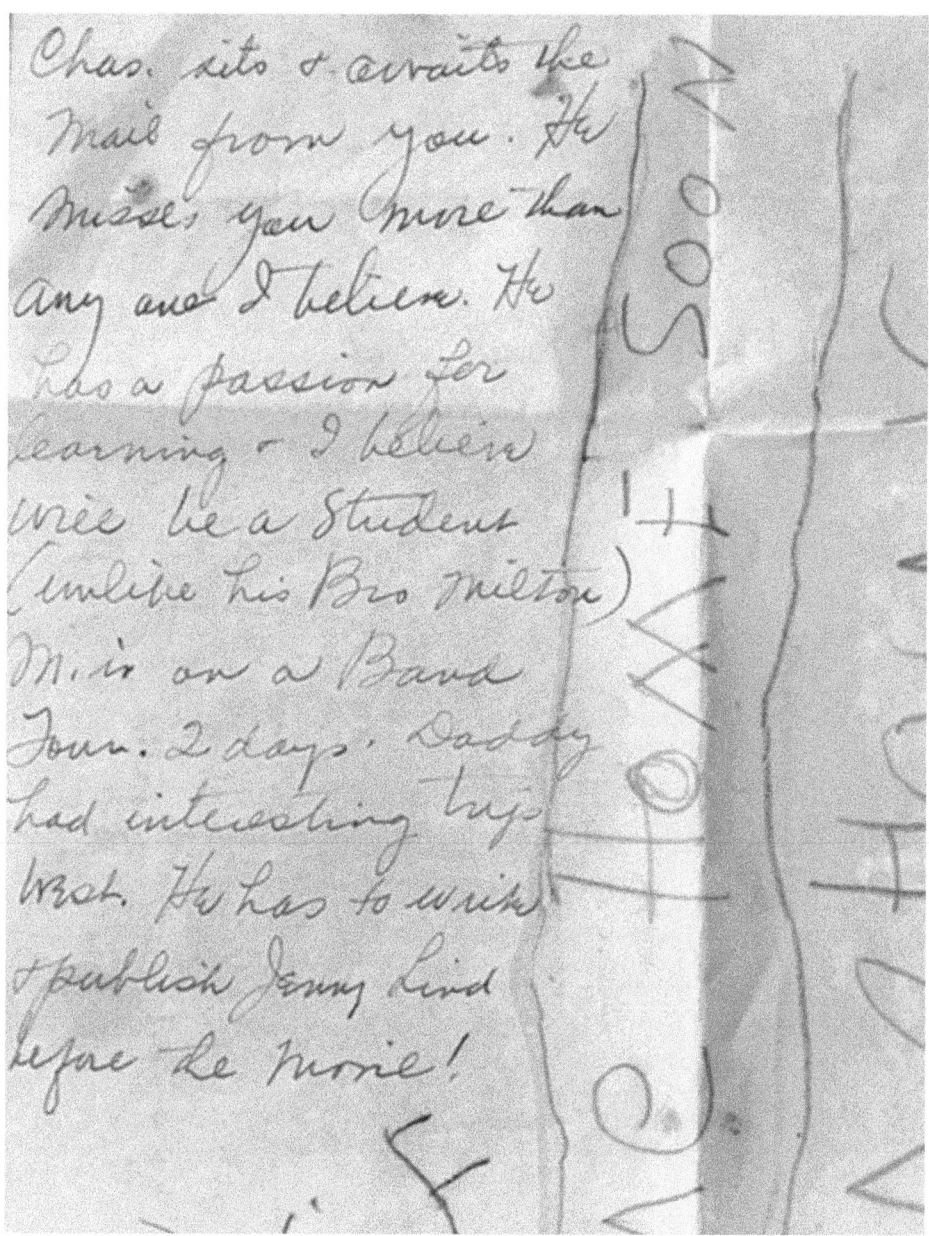

INDEX

A

A.A. Murphree, 26
America First, 62, 63
Anadarcia Sirianni, 39, 175
Angus, 9, 10, 11

B

Barry Goldwater, 152
Billy Graham, 153, 155
Boy Scout Magazine, 33
Boys' Life, 2

C

Calvin, xii, 29
Camp Clark, 9
Camp Sill, 9
Charles Augustus Lindbergh, 1, 176
Charles Lindbergh Armstrong, iv, vi, 171
Chiang Kai-shek, 121
Christian, 41, 61
Cold War, 126
communism, 114, 125, 127, 128, 130, 134

Communist, 96, 97, 99, 100, 106, 109, 111, 113, 114, 126, 127, 128, 158, 160, 164
Congressman Roy Blunt, 47
Coolidge, 29, 33
Crooked River, 49, 52
Cumberland University, 1

D

Dean Pike, 11
Dean Williams, 26
Dr. Durward Hall, 77
Dr. Durward Hall., 77
Dr. Thomas P. Sweeney, 46
Drury College, 1

E

Edwin Dorn, 66
Eisenhower, 132

F

Formosa, 111
Frank Robertson, 30

Fujikawa, 57

G

General John K. Singlaub, 160

Green New Deal, viii

Greene County, 50

Gromyko, 138

H

Halsey, 65

Hitler, 62, 65, 67, 70, 71, 104

House of Representatives, 107

Huey P. Long, 55

I

Indians, 55, 56

J

Japan, 61, 64, 66, 74, 103, 106, 107, 109, 118, 120, 130, 137, 138

John D. Rockefeller, 55

John W. Heisman, 55

K

Kansas City, 91, 92, 147, 148

Kay, vi, xi, 39, 53, 76, 79, 86, 137, 141, 175, 177

Khrushchev, 158

Kimmel, 65

Kissinger, 157, 163

Korean war, 96, 103, 106, 107, 164

L

Le Havre, 10

Louise Armstrong, 75

Louise McCool, 41, 142

Lt. Gen. Joseph Harold Moore, 161

M

MacArthur, 72, 100, 102, 104, 105, 109, 112, 116, 118, 119, 121, 122, 123, 164

Madam Chiang Kai-shek, 121

Marjorie, 85, 86, 87, 88, 94, 141, 142, 143, 144, 145, 147, 161

Millennial, viii

Milton, 26, 27, 53, 141

Missouri House of Representatives, 57

Monroe Doctrine, 125

Mother, 75, 80, 178

Mrs. Holsinger, 81

N

Negroes, 13

No Foreign War, 62, 63

North Korea, 99, 101, 104, 113, 116, 118, 131

O

Orland K. Armstrong, xii

Orville Wright, 55

P

Pearl Harbor, 53, 65, 66, 67, 68, 69, 72

Pendergast, 91, 92, 147

petroleum, 169

President Johnson, 106, 162

Pusan, 101

R

Reader's Digest, 140

Reader's Digest, 52, 71, 78, 88, 105, 139

Red China, 106, 108, 110, 111, 112, 118, 126

Richard E. Byrd, 55

Richard Nixon, 55, 159

Ridgway, 102

S

Saturday Evening Post, 51

Second World War, 70, 107, 133

Short, 65, 148

Southern Baptist Convention, 153

Soviet Union, 93, 97, 100, 125, 129, 131, 132, 138, 164

Springfield News-Leader, 50, 148

Spruance, 65

Stalin, 127

Stan, 81, 86, 88

Stanley, 64, 68, 76, 88, 144

Stimson, 66, 72

summa cum laude, 1

T

Taiwan, 119

Terasake, 64, 68

Tet Offensive, 162

The Armstrong Clan, xi

The Fifteen Decisive Battles of the United States, 96

The Journalist's Creed, 166

The Propeller, 13

Thomas B. McGuire Jr, 73

Truman, 122

U

U.S. Ambassador Joseph Kennedy, 70

U.S. Army Air Corps, 71

U.S. House of Representatives for Missouri, 2
United Nations, 98, 100, 103, 108, 109, 112, 114, 126, 131
University of Florida, 1, 26, 27, 29, 34, 39, 51, 175
University of Missouri, 1, 25, 121
University of Missouri at Columbia School of Journalism, 165

W

Walter Williams, 1, 25
Westmoreland, 161
White House, 72, 123
Will Rogers Jr., 93
William Jennings Bryan Dorn, 98
Wilson's Creek National Battlefield, 47
World War I, 13, 16, 70, 106, 119

Lightning Source UK Ltd.
Milton Keynes UK
UKHW010218141020
371524UK00004B/292